Roses
Salv
Hydrangea

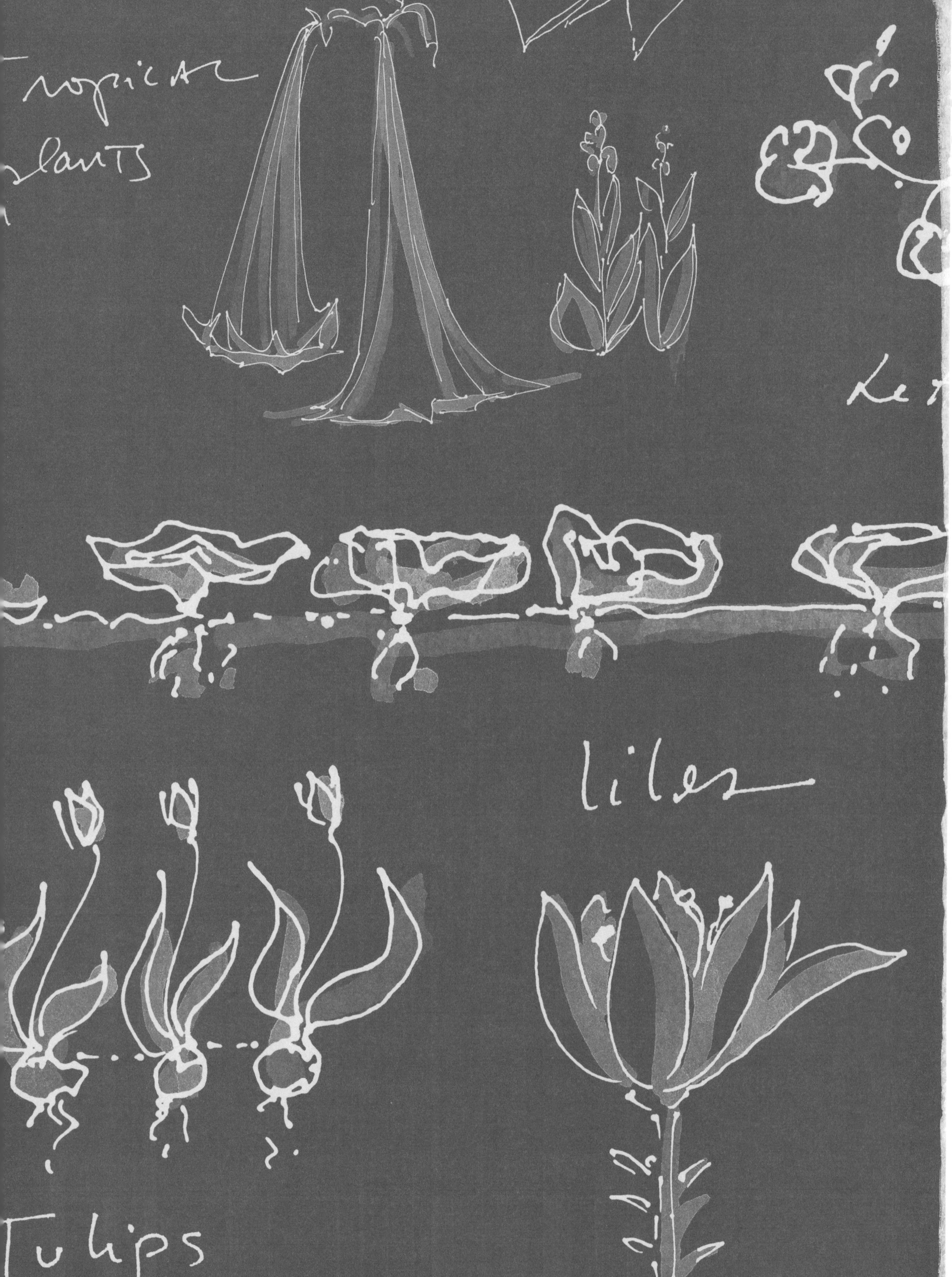
Tropical
liles
Tulips

P. Allen Smith's

LIVING IN THE GARDEN HOME

P. Allen Smith's

LIVING IN THE GARDEN HOME

Connecting the Seasons with
Containers, Crafts, and Celebrations

PHOTOGRAPHS BY JANE COLCLASURE AND KELLY QUINN
DESIGN BY DINA DELL'ARCIPRETE/DK DESIGN PARTNERS INC.

CLARKSON POTTER/PUBLISHERS
NEW YORK

Published in the United States by
Clarkson Potter/Publishers, an imprint
of the Crown Publishing Group,
a division of Random House, Inc.,
New York.
www.crownpublishing.com
www.clarksonpotter.com

Clarkson N. Potter is a trademark and
Potter and colophon are registered trademarks of
Random House, Inc.

Library of Congress Cataloging-in-Publication Data
Smith, P. Allen.
P. Allen Smith's living in the garden home: connecting
the seasons with containers, crafts, and celebrations /
P. Allen Smith ; photographs by Jane Colclasure and
Kelly Quinn.-1st ed.
1. Gardening. 2. Seasons. I. Title.
SB450.97.S65 2005
635—dc22 2007020998
ISBN 978-0-307-34723-7
Printed in Japan

10 9 8 7 6 5 4 3 2 1

First Edition

To Mom

contents

I'm often asked what inspired my passion for gardening.

I suppose the easy answer would be that I grew up with gardeners and their dedication to plants and horticulture influenced me immensely. Generations of my family have been involved in the nursery business in one form or another for more than a century. So part of the answer is that gardening is in my blood. The rest of the answer isn't so easily explained.

While I can fondly recollect my many childhood experiences centered around the garden (especially home-cooked meals made from fresh produce), there is something more than a memory that tugs at me each spring. All it takes is the slightest hint of warm air after a long cold spell to lure me outside with shovel in hand to turn over the earth, kneel down, and plant a seed. I simply can't imagine a spring any other way.

It's hard to explain why my need to grow plants is so strong, but it seems to have something to do with the act of creating. In addition to gardening, one of my other passions is plein air painting, which is painting outdoors in natural light. When I take a brush in hand with a palette of colors and lay marks on a canvas to create a picture, it sparks my inventive spirit. I feel connected to the scene before me, as if I'm serving as a conduit between what I see, the movements of my brush on the canvas, and the painting that appears.

As I garden, that sense of being a link in an act of creation is amplified. Instead of a narrow range of colors and limited ways to paint a canvas, Mother Nature provides the ultimate paint box with countless styles of three-dimensional backgrounds and inexhaustible ways to arrange the elements. But what fascinates me even more than creating art on a grand scale is that gardening also adds the factor of surprise. Unlike a painting, the scene on a garden's canvas never remains the same. Plants grow; change their shape, color, and size; and cycle through the seasons in ways that can't always be anticipated. So as I garden, there is this intangible quality of mystery and an element of the unknown that works right along with me influencing the final picture. Truth be told, there are no final pictures in gardening; just dynamic scenes set into motion, with each season revealing something new and unexpected.

I've come to think of gardening as a way to partner with nature. It's a joint venture in which we both share a measure of influence. As I move around piles of soil, build structures, and select places

RIGHT *Surely pleasure and beauty were born in the garden. Amid colorful blooms and enticing aromas I gather a bouquet of flowers to enjoy indoors.* **BELOW** *As darkness sweeps away the light, the garden is transformed, taking on a magical quality in the glow of twilight.* **BELOW RIGHT** *Much of the enjoyment of gardening comes through the sense of touch. Handling plants, seeds, soil, and tools is a rich part of the experience.*

for the plants, nature does her part in supporting my efforts, and, on occasion, she bursts in to completely redesign my plans and remind me of who's actually in charge. Working with such a dynamic force is a big part of what feeds my insatiable desire to pick up a shovel and, come what may, try again. Every time I do, I gain respect for nature's power and the ancient rhythms revealed in each seasonal cycle. It's a humbling reminder that despite my best efforts, I'm never really in control of anything.

Sometimes when I can work uninterrupted in the garden, I find that the simplest tasks have a subtle and calming effect on my state of mind. Watering one container and then the next is mesmerizing. The repetition of chipping, mowing, or turning the soil and certainly deadheading can set into place a cadence that anchors me in the moment. When I am transfixed on these activities, the rest of the world falls away and I find myself in an almost meditative state.

Gardening gives me so much: The anticipation of a new season, the promise of all it holds, the mystery of not knowing, the surprise when things change, the challenge of overcoming obstacles, the chance to learn something new, the amazement in seeing things grow, the satisfaction when combinations come together, the heartbreak when they fall apart, all these elements play a part in replenishing the deep well of pleasure that I gain in the process.

How about you? What draws you outside to plant, battle weeds, brave the weather, and then fall into a chair at the end of the day with a contented sigh? Whether you are sure of your answer or are still trying to figure it out, this book is grist for the mill. I offer it to all those who feel the desire to plant a seed and then have the patience to wait and see what happens. It is a compendium—part journal, part project guide—that walks you through a year of seasons in my garden to reveal how deeply this calling is woven into the fabric of my life. The garden is more than a place outside the walls of my house that I plant each spring and then abandon in the fall. My garden rooms are extensions of my living space and are just as much a part of my home as the rooms inside. Spending time in the garden is the way I stay connected to nature and renew my ongoing partnership with her. I grow plants for food and for pleasure. One nourishes my body, the other my soul. I need both to feel complete. And so the full answer to the question of why I garden comes down to this: I do it because I must. My hope is that by sharing my seasonal journey, you, too, will discover some new reasons why you must garden, and along the way create many seasons filled with your own garden pleasures.

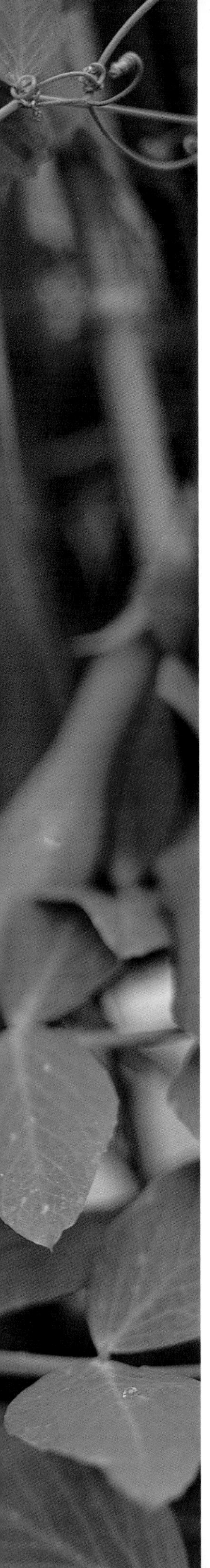

spring.

Riding high on a wave of great hopes and big plans, I eagerly anticipate all that spring offers to a passionate gardener. You will see what I mean as you read about all the projects I have selected for this season. After winter's repose, each plant holds the promise of what this year's garden can be. The rising energy of the season is unmistakable and I feel its strong current within me. Like sentinels on watch, the early daffodils sound out the first note of spring. As the flowering shrubs of witch hazel, forsythia, and quince bloom and 'Okame' cherry trees unfold, the crescendo builds. Soon, red maple flowers, redbuds, tulips, and viburnums join in the chorus until all the colors of spring are singing together. It's hard not to get caught up in the grand concert of unparalleled excitement and beauty.

As the plants emerge and shake off their drab winter colors, the sun warms the earth and the sweet scent of spring fills the air. Familiar aromas such as newly mown grass, spring rain, fresh-tilled soil, and those first fragile flowers carry with them a flood of delightful memories.

In early spring, before things really kick into high gear, I survey the garden to see what I might do to make my tasks a little easier. Over the past few years, I've found myself looking for a place to pot up plants or store often-used supplies as I'm working in my vegetable garden. To remedy the situation, I built a fold-down shelf for the side of my toolshed. Like my favorite pair of pocket pruners, this handy work surface is conveniently close by whenever I need it.

As I work outside, I can appreciate the beauty of my first daffodils. I enjoy these spring flowering bulbs so much I have planted early-, mid-, and late-season bloomers to extend their flowering time as long as possible. I love cutting armloads of daffodils to bring into the house.

Another spring ritual I look forward to each year is planting a new rose. I plant roses everywhere I can: Many of the borders in my garden are filled with old-fashioned shrub roses, climbing roses accent my arbors and toolshed, and compact varieties adorn several containers. Their allure is irresistible and I always seem to find one more that I must add to my collection.

Spring is the time to start some plants as seeds indoors. It's a great way to grow varieties that I can't find in the local nursery or ones that I want to get a head start on in the garden. Others I sow directly outside. After winter I'm always eager to taste my first spring salad, so as soon as the weather allows, I plant a variety of greens in my vegetable garden. Cool temperatures and frequent rains are the ideal growing conditions.

While I'm cleaning up the flower beds, I'm careful to avoid emerging plants. Last summer, I let some of my annual flowers develop into seed pods and they scattered their seeds throughout the bed. I can't be sure where these hearty volunteers may pop up, so I watch for their tiny seedlings among the perennials.

Until spring temperatures even out, I busy myself by planting lots of containers. Creating mini-gardens full of flowers, fruits, vegetables, and herbs satisfies my urge to plant every piece of bare ground. I also look forward to creating a Mother's Day container filled with beautiful flowers and foliage as a gift for all the special women in my life.

Once the last frost date has passed, I kick into high gear. I sow seeds for my cut flower garden, plant new varieties of perennials and annuals, and then cross my fingers that this will be the year that everything grows just as I imagined. By the time my peonies bloom at the end of the spring season, my dream is becoming a glorious reality.

CLOCKWISE FROM ABOVE RIGHT *Starting seeds in labeled pots creates a mini-nursery. 'Narragansett' crabapples frame a tulip and pansy border in my rondel garden. Bright blue and white violas dance behind pots of young sweet peas and nasturtiums. A lively mix of 'Perestroyka' and 'Temple of Beauty' tulips, 'Giant Red Mustard', curled parsley, dinosaur kale, blue pansies, and pots of 'Sugar Snap' peas, lettuce, and arugula fill my spring vegetable garden.*

The Budding Garden

"While the daffodils bloom" signifies a time in early spring when I gather my garden tools, clean containers, replenish supplies, and get my equipment in order so everything will be handy and ready to use. I feel all set when I have a stockpile of bagged soil mixes in the tubs under my potting bench, a mound of mulch piled up next to my potting shed, and a fresh supply of fertilizers, insecticidal soap, and items needed for my weekend projects. It's so much easier to get enthused about working in the garden when my time isn't interrupted with running to the store for last-minute supplies.

If I followed my own advice last fall and cleaned and put away my garden tools, I'd be in pretty good shape. If not, now's the time to do that. A quick inventory lets me know what needs to be sharpened, has to be replaced, or may be missing-in-action. I'm bad about leaving tools in the garden. To help me find them, I give the handles a quick shot of a fluorescent-colored spray paint or wrap them with brightly colored tape. I've tried the hanging-every-tool-on-the-wall approach of organizing things, but I've discovered that I'm more of a toss-the-hand-tools-in-a-plastic-bucket-by-the-door kind of guy. Whatever works is my motto. And who hasn't been in the garden, knee deep in a project, when the phone rings? Recently I've been using a gardener's phone belt that keeps my cell phone, pruners, and other items close at hand. Another simple and lightweight helper is a 5-gallon bucket. It's great for hauling tools and supplies and toting weeds to the compost pile. And when my knees need a break, I turn it upside down and use it as a sturdy seat.

ABOVE *A sturdy table with a durable surface is perfect for potting up containers.* **LEFT** *A simple pegged board helps me stay organized.* **OPPOSITE** *A well-stocked potting bench is as satisfying as a full pantry.*

Stow-away potting bench

The beauty of this bench design is that the surface is connected to the wall with hinges. This means you can fold it up so it's out of the way when you don't need it, or let it down and simply attach the corners to sturdy chains to create a readily accessible workspace. If you'd like to build a version of my potting bench, just follow the instructions below and attach the bench to any sturdy vertical surface near your garden such as a fence, side of the garage, potting shed, or house. For some extra storage, I added a shelf and pegged board above the bench. If you don't feel comfortable using a hammer and saw, you can give the plans to a carpenter or a handy helper.

Since this bench will be used outside, choose weather-resistant lumber such as Western red cedar. All fasteners such as screws, nails, and hinges should be galvanized or coated for exterior use. The materials and supplies are for one 65-inch-long workbench. You can adjust the measurements to fit your particular needs and location.

materials

(2) 65-inch-long 2 x 4-inch boards

(5) 15-inch-long 2 x 4-inch boards

(6) 65-inch-long 1 x 3-inch boards (or 67 inches long if you prefer an overhang on the side ends of the workbench)

(2) 75-inch-long heavyweight chains

(4) heavy-gauge screw hooks

(2) 4-inch heavy-duty galvanized hinges

(1) box of 1½-inch decking screws

(25) 1½-inch finishing nails

Nail set

Level

Small bolt cutters (to cut chain to finished length)

Hammer, screwdriver, electric skill saw

1. Create a frame for the workbench's top by taking one 65-inch-long 2 x 4 and, starting at one end, drilling five evenly spaced holes down its length every 13 inches. Next, attach the five 15-inch boards to the longer board, screwing the five boards in place from the outside in. Using the same method, attach the second 65-inch board to the 15-inch boards to complete the frame. You will now have a rectangle that stands 3½ inches high on all sides.

2. Assemble the bench top by laying out the six 1 x 3 boards, spacing them ¾ inch apart. Make sure that the back outer piece is flush to the back edge of the frame. The front outer piece will hang over the edge about ¾ inch. Secure these boards with finishing nails, using a nail set to sink the nail heads just below the surface.

3. Attach two screw hooks at the front of each end of the bench. Predrill and attach the heavyweight hinges to the back of the shelf. Get some help to hold the top against the wall to determine a comfortable standing height for the workbench and mark for the placement of the hinges, then attach the bench to the wall with screws.

4. Attach a length of chain to each screw hook on the bench top. With a helper holding the bench parallel to the ground, determine where to place the last two screw hooks in the wall. Use a level to ensure that the table lies flat. Mark and attach the last two screw hooks to the wall. Cut the chain as needed.

SIGNATURE PLANT

1. 'Ice King'
2. 'Avalanche'
3. 'Sailboat'
4. 'Pipit'
5. 'Professor Einstein'
6. 'Yellow Cheerfulness'
7. 'Pheasant's Eye'
8. 'Stratosphere'
9. 'Thalia'

Daffodils

Whose heart doesn't leap upon seeing that first daffodil in the spring? What a delight! I can't imagine my garden without them. They are perhaps the most carefree flowers I grow. While I don't like to play favorites, daffodils are at the top of my list of spring-flowering bulbs because of their simple beauty and reliable nature. You'll need to plant these spring bloomers in the fall, but it's worth the wait to see their cheery flowers, which are deer resistant, can be grown almost anywhere, and come in a beautiful range of colors and styles. You may know this plant by one of its common names—buttercup, Lent lily, or jonquil. Even *daffodil* is a common name—its proper Latin, or botanical, name is *Narcissus.* Call them what you will, by any name they are a welcome sign that spring has arrived.

1.
2.
3.
4.
5.
6.
7.
8.
9.

CLOCKWISE FROM RIGHT *Show off daffodils by gathering seven or eight blooms, cutting the stems off evenly, and then loosely binding the flowers together with a rubber band positioned just under the blooms; line up several mini-bouquets in matching vases. A gorgeous fan of 'Manly' daffodils creates a stunning display. Each year I add more daffodils to my garden to make sure I'll have plenty for arrangements.* **OPPOSITE** *Single stems of 'Geranium' daffodils are held aloft next to a mix of 'Sir Winston Churchill', 'Yellow Cheerfulness', and more 'Geranium' daffodils.*

NO BLOOMS? THE PROBLEM COULD BE:

1. Too much shade—daffodils prefer full sun.
2. Overcrowding—the bulbs multiply and they need to be dug up, separated, and replanted anytime they become crowded or flower production decreases.
3. Wrong planting depth—the rule of thumb is plant them at a depth three times the height of the bulb.
4. Foliage removed too soon—leaves need 6 to 8 weeks to recharge the bulb.

Dazzling Daffodil Arrangements

Few things brighten a room more than a vase of daffodils. As soon as they bloom in my garden, I cut a big bouquet to bring inside. But before you gather and arrange the flowers, there are some things you should know. When you cut a daffodil, there is a sap that flows from its hollow stem. Compounds in the sap cause other flowers, when used in the same arrangement with daffodils, to wilt. To avoid this problem I create all-daffodil bouquets, but if you are more patient than I am, you can set the flowers aside for 12 hours in a separate container. Change the water a couple of times to remove the sap before mixing them with other flowers.

A simple and elegant daffodil arrangement can be made by gathering several blooms of one variety, trimming their stems to 4 to 5 inches, and securing them with a rubber band near the flower heads, where it can't be seen.

To display longer-stemmed daffodils, I create a simple holder by bending a small piece of chicken wire to fit into the top of a vase or container. The spaces between the wire allow the flowers to be positioned in any direction. Conceal the holder by filling in between the flowers with an evergreen, like the classic boxwood. The dark green color also helps to set off the blooms.

Daffodil Maintenance

Along with enjoying the flowers inside your home, you can help daffodil bulbs recover and bloom again next spring by removing the spent blossoms, applying about a tablespoon of a well-balanced fertilizer such as 20-20-20 or 13-13-13 around each plant, and leaving the foliage and stems intact for at least 6 to 8 weeks after the flowers fade in order to recharge the bulbs.

If you have daffodils that need relocating, spring is a good time to transplant them. The foliage rejuvenates the bulbs after transplanting, so make sure that the foliage stays attached.

Putting Down Roots

With my tools sharpened and my inventory of supplies replenished, I'm ready to take on one of my favorite projects: planting a bare-root rose. Roses can be purchased three different ways: grown in containers, wrapped in loose material inside a poly bag, or bare-root. Although each will produce fine roses, I lean toward bare-root stock because I'm always on the prowl for a good buy. Bare-root roses cost much less than container-grown plants because they are stored in a dormant state without soil. If the roots are kept moist with wet burlap, shredded paper, or sawdust and in cool conditions, the plant does just fine. When planted in early spring, bare-root roses adjust well to new soil and garden conditions. And since most plant catalogs ship roses bare-root, you often find a wider selection of varieties available through mail-order sources.

Roses can also be sold as either own-root or grafted stock. There is some debate over which is better. Own-root roses are propagated by rooting stem cuttings of one variety of rose, whereas grafted bare-root roses are stem cuttings of one variety of rose budded onto year-old field-grown rootstocks of another variety such as 'Dr. Huey' for faster propagation. Northern gardeners have told me that own-root roses have a better chance of survival during severe winters as they can freeze to the ground and still spring back from their roots and bloom the following summer. They also tend to be truer to type than budded roses, which may revert to their rootstock, resulting in blooms from the rootstock rather than from the chosen variety grafted above.

If you are buying from a local garden center or nursery, choose a plant with at least three strong canes and avoid those with brown, shriveled, diseased, or damaged branches and roots. Some plants are sold with canes that have been dipped in paraffin, but I've never had much luck with those. Examine the plants for brightly colored buds on the sides of the stems; this is a good sign that the plant is alive and well and will come to life at the first sign of a warm day.

When planting roses, pay particular attention to where you place them. Most, unless they are shade-tolerant varieties, need to be located in an area that gets 4 to 6 hours of direct sunlight a day and plenty of air circulation. This will cut down on fungal problems later in the season.

LEFT *I prepare my flower beds for spring planting by turning over the soil and adding generous amounts of compost.* **OPPOSITE** *'New Dawn' roses blanket this archway, creating an inviting entrance to a quiet sitting area. Roses add such a romantic quality to any setting that I always try to find room for one more in my garden each spring.*

Rose Soil Recipe

Adding roses to my garden is one of my most satisfying and rewarding spring projects. If you want some ideas of varieties of roses to plant in your garden, get a sneak peek on pages 64–69, where I share a list of some of my favorites. Roses thrive in a rich loam that's well drained. If you have less than desirable soil for roses, try my rose soil recipe; it has never failed me!

materials

(2) buckets of existing garden soil (from the hole you're digging)
(½) bucket of organic manure
(1) bucket of compost
(½) cup of greensand* (optional)
(1) tablespoon of Epsom salts (for added magnesium)
(2) chopped-up banana peels (for added potassium)
Fish emulsion (follow label directions)

*Greensand is an organic fertilizer composed primarily of iron-potassium silicate. I like to use it because not only does it give plants a boost, it will also help improve soil texture and drainage. I have had the best luck finding greensand locally at a farmer's co-op, or you can buy it online or through the mail from organic garden-supply companies such as Gardener's Supply Company (see Source Guide, page 209).

1. The day before planting, soak the rose overnight in a bucket of tepid water to rehydrate it. Avoid leaving it in the water for more than a day.

2. Dig a planting hole that's at least wide enough for you to spread all of the roots out and about 14 to 18 inches deep. Place banana peels in the bottom of the planting hole.

3. Blend all ingredients except the banana peels and fish emulsion in a wheelbarrow.

4. Pay attention to the placement of the bud union (the swollen part of the plant between the roots and limbs, where the rose variety you've chosen has been grafted onto a hardy rootstock) if you are planting a grafted or budded type rose. If you live in an area where winters are extremely cold, you'll want to bury it approximately 1 to 2 inches below the surface of the ground for protection. In milder parts of the country, you can plant the rose with the bud union roughly 1 to 1½ inches above ground level.

5. Once the rose is placed at the correct level for your climate, begin filling the hole with the rose soil mixture, gently tamping the soil around the roots. After the hole has been filled, water the rose well to help settle the soil. Give the plant a little extra boost with a solution of fish emulsion. (Follow the directions on the bottle.)

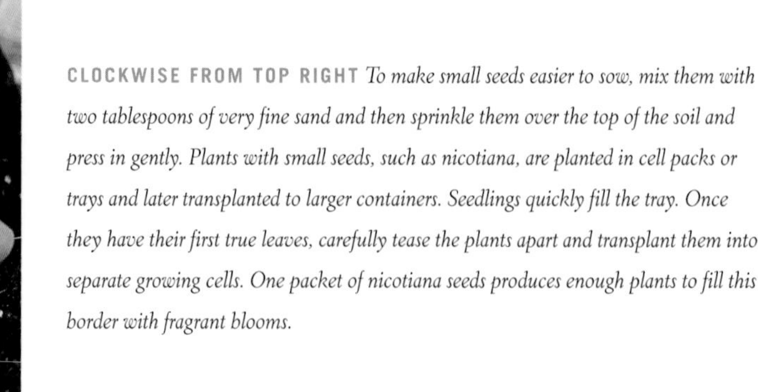

CLOCKWISE FROM TOP RIGHT *To make small seeds easier to sow, mix them with two tablespoons of very fine sand and then sprinkle them over the top of the soil and press in gently. Plants with small seeds, such as nicotiana, are planted in cell packs or trays and later transplanted to larger containers. Seedlings quickly fill the tray. Once they have their first true leaves, carefully tease the plants apart and transplant them into separate growing cells. One packet of nicotiana seeds produces enough plants to fill this border with fragrant blooms.*

Starting Seeds Indoors

Planting seeds is a rite of spring I always enjoy. Being thrifty at heart, I take great pleasure in paying a few dollars for a packet of seeds and getting a whole bed of flowers or vegetables in return. Whenever I shake a few seeds into my hand, it doesn't seem possible that with a little soil, water, and time, these tiny specks will transform themselves into something glorious. It's an amazing process that I regard as nothing less than a miracle.

Along with the cost savings, growing plants from seed is a way to include unique varieties or special colors in the garden that may not be available at the local nursery. It's also a way for me to get a jump on spring. Once the weather breaks, my indoor-grown seedlings will be sturdy and strong enough to be transplanted into the garden.

Gardeners have many ways of approaching the process of starting seeds indoors. Many keep precise records, buy indoor lights and stands, and follow time-honored methods. You can make it as simple or as complex as you want. There are seed-starting kits that will walk you through each step and provide you with all the needed materials, but I've found that the following guidelines are all I've ever needed for successful germination.

- Check the seed packets to make sure the seeds were packaged for the current growing season.
- Recycle nursery cell packs and other wide, flat containers such as margarine tubs to start seedlings. Plastic pots retain moisture more consistently than clay ones do.
- Sanitize containers by soaking them in a 10 percent bleach solution for 20 minutes, let them air-dry, and poke drainage holes in the bottom.
- Use a soilless seed-starting mix to fill containers. Place seeds on the surface, then use a kitchen sieve to shake more mix on top. Usually a light covering, no more than twice their diameter, is sufficient. Gently press the top of the mix so the seeds and mix make contact.
- While some seeds require total darkness to germinate, others require light. Many varieties will germinate in either situation. The seed packet should tell you what that variety's requirements are. For those that need light, press seeds into the soil mix without covering with soil. Professional growers often use a dusting of vermiculite to help keep the seeds moist and in position without excluding light.
- Spritz the surface with water from a spray bottle and cover with plastic wrap to keep the soil moisture constant until the seeds germinate. Check the soil daily.
- Keep seeds warm (65 to 75 degrees F) by placing them on a seed heating pad or in a warm location.
- Once the seeds germinate, remove the plastic and provide good air circulation to prevent fungal infection. Keep the soil moist but not soggy. If your seeds didn't require light to germinate, once they sprout they will need light to develop into strong, healthy plants.
- If you've set the seed flats in front of a window, turn the seedlings daily to keep the stems strong.
- Once the second set of leaves has developed, feed the seedlings weekly with a half-strength liquid fertilizer.
- Harden the seedlings for transplanting. The first day, place the seedlings outside in a shady, protected area for a few hours, and then increase sun exposure gradually each day for a week.

SIGNATURE PLANT

1. 'Freckles' lettuce
2. 'Pot of Gold', 'Scarlet Charlotte', and 'Silver Rib' Swiss chard
3. 'Eruption' lettuce
4. Radishes, 'Kyuna Myzuna' mustard, claytonia, minutina, and 'Little Gem' lettuce
5. 'Deer Tongue' lettuce
6. Rustic, Italian, and 'Runway' arugula
7. 'Jericho' lettuce
8. 'Rainbow' Swiss chard
9. 'Salad Bowl' lettuce

Salad Greens

Salad greens are among the easiest and most rewarding plants to grow. Simple, sweet, and tasty, these cool-season plants seem completely undaunted even as the turbulent winds of early spring howl around them. They have few needs; with just a light dusting of soil over the seeds, sunlight, and water, they are up and growing in no time. They are friendly plants that mix and mingle easily; I've found that you can plant them almost anywhere—in vegetable gardens, alongside tulips in flower beds, even nestled into containers or window boxes.

1.
2.
3.
4.
5.
6.
7.
8.
9.

Sprout an Interest in Gardening

Here's a project that's fun to do with children. Hyacinth bean vines and gourds are easy-to-grow, annual climbers that will capture a child's imagination. The seeds sprout quickly and the vines readily cover fences, arbors, and trellises in one season. Fragrant purple or white pea-blossom-shaped flowers of the hyacinth bean vines open in late summer and are followed by velvety, deep purple seedpods. And the gourds produce wacky, colorful fruits that make fun projects in the fall.

Although you can sow the seeds directly in the garden after the danger of frost has passed, I like to start mine indoors so they'll be ready to take off and cover a fence once it's warm enough to plant them out in my garden.

I start the seedlings about four weeks before the date I plan to plant them outdoors. For containers, I use anything I have on hand, such as small 4-inch peat pots or clean and sterilized nursery trays from the previous year. Any small, waterproof container with drainage holes will do. Fill the seed holders about halfway with a bagged seed-starter mix. These blends have been designed to give seedlings a quick start, so don't be tempted to use soil from the garden or yard.

Place 1 seed per pot and cover it with roughly 1 inch of soil. Water and put the pots in a warm, sunny area. Keep the soil moist and in about 10 to 15 days, you will see the plants emerge. As the vines begin to grow, turn the containers each day so the plants won't lean toward the light.

Once the seedlings are 6 to 8 inches tall and the threat of frost has passed, you can plant them outside. For tips on how to transplant and train them to climb up a simple string trellis, see page 80.

While the hyacinth beans are getting a head start indoors, I've already turned over the soil in my vegetable garden and started my cool-season crops. When soil temperatures are consistently in the 50-degree F range, you can safely plant most spring vegetable seeds. Even then, I wait until after a rain, when the soil is crumbly, and work in any needed amendments, such as compost and organic fertilizers. Designating plants as either cool or warm season has less to do with the time of year a certain vegetable should be planted than with the temperature needed for optimum growth. Cool-season vegetables—including most salad greens, peas, onions, radishes, and carrots as well as cabbage, cauliflower, and broccoli—can tolerate temperatures slightly below freezing, so they are the first to be planted. Their warm-season counterparts—tomatoes, corn, peppers, eggplant, squash, and melons—may die if air temperatures drop below 50 degrees F, so you'll need to wait to plant those until warm weather has set in. My first spring vegetable plantings are usually salad greens because they thrive in cooler temperatures. I can't wait to enjoy that first spring salad.

LEFT *I like to start large seeds for plants like 'Ruby Moon' hyacinth bean vines in 3-inch peat pots. When the plants are ready to grow outside, I just gently tear away the bottom and place the entire pot directly in the prepared bed.*
OPPOSITE *Few things taste better than just-picked salad greens fresh from the garden.*

RIGHT *Grow fresh salad greens in a sunny spot just outside your kitchen door.* **BELOW RIGHT** *The colorful foliage of 'Buttercrunch' and 'Red Sails' lettuce complements the blooms of spring flowering tulips.* **BELOW LEFT** *Use scissors to harvest the top few inches of cut-and-come-again mesclun mix. They'll offer up new leaves in about a week.*

Growing Great Greens

The lettuces that you may be most familiar with are the iceberg and green- or red-leafed varieties found in produce aisles. But there are hundreds of other greens—including mustard, spinach, endive, radicchio, beet, parsley, mâche, and cresses—that can add delectable flavor and color to your salads.

Growing your own greens lets you try new and exciting varieties, and if you plant the seeds early in cold frames, you can enjoy fresh greens long before most plants in the garden even emerge. In fact, greens grow best in the cool, rainy days of early spring and late fall.

Some gardeners grow each variety of salad green separately in rows or in containers, while others try combining four or five different kinds to create mesclun, a seasonal mixture of greens grown and harvested together. You can easily create your own mix with a variety of leaf lettuces and other greens, or you can purchase premixed seed packets.

To enjoy a continuous supply of greens through the spring and early summer, sow a handful of seeds every 10 days or so. As the temperatures climb, even those varieties of lettuce that are "slow to bolt" may become leathery and tough. Each variety has its own sensitivity to the heat, so to tell if your lettuce is bitter, taste a leaf. To avoid serving up a salad of overly bitter greens, sow your final plantings two months before the maximum daytime temperatures average 80 degrees F.

Here are some of my favorite salad greens and the number of days it takes to grow them to maturity.

'BUTTERCRUNCH' (65 days) This large, heat-resistant butterhead-type lettuce is one of my all-time favorites. It truly does have a buttery velvetlike flavor that surpasses that of most lettuce varieties. It grows as a loose head with smooth, ruffled green leaves and a yellow-white compact center or heart.

'RED SAILS' (45 days) This looseleaf lettuce variety is ready to eat in no time. The red and light green rippled leaves make a colorful addition to any salad, and it stands in the garden a long time after maturity without bolting or becoming bitter.

'JERICHO' ROMAINE (55 to 65 days) A heat-tolerant lettuce that retains its sweet flavor and crisp yet juicy texture even with lapses in watering and spikes in temperature. Large heads with sword-shaped leaves make this a popular choice among salad lovers.

'RED ERUPTION' BIBB-ROMAINE (50 days) Add bursts of color to your garden and plate with this intensely red-colored mini Bibb-romaine lettuce. The glossy, savory leaves are crisp and mild tasting.

'SALAD BOWL' GREEN OAKLEAF (48 days) This is an old-time favorite leaf lettuce that dates from the 1880s. The thin, light green, oak-leaf-shaped leaves form tight rosettes. Heat-resistant, these plants last for weeks after numerous cuttings.

'DEER TONGUE' GREEN BIBB (45 to 55 days) This looseleaf lettuce variety has been a favorite for years because of its heavy production and dependability. The green, triangular leaves grow on thick, solid plants and have a pleasantly sharp flavor.

ARUGULA (40 days) The king of gourmet salad greens, arugula's dark lobed leaves have a sharp, "peppery" taste and form an open head. For best taste, harvest the leaves when they are 2 to 3 inches tall.

MALABAR SPINACH (45 to 55 days) While not a true spinach, this climbing plant has a similar taste and is ideal for containers and small gardens because it can be grown vertically, taking up little garden space. Sometimes used for its ornamental qualities, it produces large, dark green leaves and vines. Try the red variety to add a touch of color to your vegetable garden. Young leaves and tips are great for stir-fry cooking. Presoaking the seed for 24 hours in warm water before planting shortens the germination time.

'RED GIANT' MUSTARD GREENS (21 to 45 days) This striking plant has a bright look and bold flavor. Zesty lime green leaves are overlaid with bright purple to go along with its delightful sweet but spicy flavor. Baby greens are ready in just 21 days for salad mixes or 45 days as a cooked green.

'BRIGHT LIGHTS' SWISS CHARD (50 to 62 days) A dazzling plant in the garden, this offers pink, red, bright gold, pale orange, white, and mauve stems holding green to bronze-green leaves. Both the stalks and the leaves can be harvested. You can prepare the stalks like celery or asparagus. The leaves can be used raw for baby green harvest or cooked with garlic or nutmeg and butter to enhance the chard's flavor.

Sweet Surprises

Tender beauty fills my garden as more plants awaken from their winter's rest. Fresh and unblemished leaves, supple stems, and fat flower buds define spring's perfection. At times like this I want to freeze the moment, so I can recall the image when my garden languishes in late summer. So many moments define the season. Sometimes, I'll be deep in thought, completely focused on a garden task, only to lift my head just as a soft ray of sunlight illuminates the water in my fountain garden or I'll catch sight of a bird gathering twigs for her nest. I'm reminded of how fleeting and magical these days in the garden are and feel lucky to be there taking them in. The more time I spend in my garden, the better I feel.

There comes a point in spring's unfolding sequence when the garden transforms itself from fledgling beds with sprigs of soft green to borders bursting with fresh vegetation. I've often wondered how my garden would appear if I just stepped back, folded my hands, and watched. It's a time when I'm reminded that some of the best gardeners are those with relaxed, easygoing personalities, the kind of people who don't obsess over details and can be content to let nature take its course in their gardens. I see this most frequently in rural gardens where the natural world takes the lead without much intrusion by human hands, producing some remarkable results.

I strive to emulate that hands-off spirit by giving over part of my garden to hardy volunteers. Although they are annuals, these plants grow, flower, and reseed themselves with such vigor that I can always count on them to come back year after year. Because the seeds fall where they may, in spring I'm surprised and delighted to see where they've sown themselves and in what magical combinations.

One of my favorite volunteers is the larkspur, which flowers at the same time as the irises, Oriental poppies, peonies, and the first blush of roses in my garden. When you combine the tall, elegant spires of larkspur with roses and perennials—well, all I can say is, flower gardening just doesn't get much better than this.

I established my first patch of larkspur by growing them from seed. I was having a little trouble getting the seeds going until I tried a trick a fellow gardener suggested. He recommended that I chill the seeds in the refrigerator for about a week before I planted them. This seemed to help improve the germination rate. I also selected a location with full sun and good drainage. Once the plants were up and flowering, I let them "roam" to other established areas of my flower beds. Sometimes I help the process along by capturing the seeds from the ripened flower heads and scattering them about.

It's important to learn to identify your volunteer seedlings so you don't pull them up as weeds. You'll also want to avoid smothering the seeds with a heavy layer of mulch, and if you use any preemergent herbicide, steer clear of the areas where the volunteers may grow.

One note of caution: For some plants, the line between hardy volunteers and invasive weeds is a fine one indeed. It's always a good idea to check with knowledgeable garden center staff or longtime gardeners in your area to make sure you know which plants to welcome into your garden.

OPPOSITE, ABOVE *'Messenger Pink' and 'Giant Imperial Lavender' larkspur bloom as a colorful, carefree mix along my picket fence.*
BELOW *Globe amaranth is a true everlasting flower. It will freely self-sow, and the dried blooms will last a long time in arrangements.*

HEARTY VOLUNTEERS IN MY GARDEN

- Bachelor's buttons (*Centaurea* spp.)
- Cosmos (*Cosmos* spp.)
- Flowering tobacco (*Nicotiana* spp.)
- Globe amaranth (*Gomphrena* spp.)
- Larkspur (*Consolida ajacis*)
- Nigella (*Nigella damascena*)
- Old-fashioned petunias (*Petunia*)
- Queen Anne's lace (*Daucus carota* spp. *carota*)
- Verbena-on-a-stick (*Verbena bonariensis*)

Celebrate the Season

mother's day—a gift of beauty

Mother's Day comes at such a splendid time of the year. As the light spreads its radiance across an ever more verdant landscape and the garden dons its flowery finest, it is the perfect moment to pause and celebrate the beauty and nurturing qualities of motherhood. A special gift that your mother, grandmother, or special female in your life will enjoy all summer long is a beautiful container garden. This simple yet stunning arrangement requires only three varieties of plants found in most nurseries, so you'll find it easy to create the same gorgeous results.

The plants I selected for this arrangement are shade loving because experience tells me that mothers like to prominently display their presents—so the container will be placed near the front or back door. Unless the entrance is south facing, the plants will be in the shade most of the day. If the gift will be displayed in a sunny location, I've listed an alternative plant combination at the end of the recipe that you can put together with equal success.

materials

(1) 18-inch-diameter terra-cotta pot

(1) 16-quart bag soilless container mix

Small jar of water-retentive polymers

Small container of slow-release fertilizer

(1) 10- to 12-inch hanging basket (or 1-gallon container) of 'Lilac Super Sonic' New Guinea impatiens

(2) 6-inch pots of 'Gloire de Marengo' variegated ivy (*Hedera algeriensis* 'Gloire de Marengo')

(2) 1-gallon Japanese painted fern (*Athyrium nipponicum* 'Pictum')

1. Use a clean 18-inch-diameter terra-cotta pot that has been soaked in water. Soaking keeps the pot from wicking water from the soil inside the container and drying the plants' roots. A wheelbarrow or a plastic tub filled with water is an easy way to soak pots. When the container is completely submerged, you'll see strings of tiny bubbles rising to the surface. When the bubbles stop, the container is saturated.

2. Cover the drainage holes in the bottom of the pot with a small piece of window screen to prevent the soil from running out; if that's not handy, add a few broken pot shards or a thin layer of gravel to the bottom of the container. A coffee filter placed over the drainage hole is another option.

3. Pour the bagged soilless mix into the pot until it is two-thirds full. If your potting soil already contains water-retentive polymers and slow-release fertilizers, you're ready to plant. If not, follow label directions and mix those ingredients into the soil.

4. Remove the impatiens from the nursery pot and place them at the back of the container. If needed add or remove some of the potting mix below the impatiens so they will sit about 1 inch below the top of the terra-cotta pot. This will give water a place to pool rather than running over the sides of the container.

continues on following pages

5. Slip the Japanese painted fern from its plastic pot and position it next to the impatiens. Arrange the variegated ivies across the front. Add soil under the plants if necessary to raise them to the same level as the impatiens. Press the soil in firmly around the plants. Water thoroughly.

6. Adjust some of the fronds of the fern to mix and mingle with the leaves and blooms of the impatiens. Then arrange the ivies so they tumble over the front edge of the container and blend in with the impatiens and the fern. The container now has a more gardenlike appearance, as if the plants have been growing together for a long time.

care instructions

The plants will grow best in a location in partial shade where it is cool or in full shade when the weather turns hot. Keep the soil moist, but not wet, feeding the plants twice a month with an all-purpose liquid fertilizer until late summer. To encourage the impatiens to maintain a full appearance, cut back leggy plants and they will rebloom in a few weeks. At the end of the summer the perennial fern can be transplanted into a shady flower border. The ivy is considered a "tender perennial" and can be used as a houseplant where winters are severe.

The super-sized lilac blooms of the New Guinea impatiens blend perfectly with the lacy hand-painted quality of the Japanese painted fern. Cascading along the front of the container is a variegated ivy called 'Gloire de Marengo'. Its glossy green leaves are edged in creamy white, adding just the right sparkle to the composition. Since you'll want the planted container to look picture perfect as soon as you assemble it, I suggest you buy large, mature-looking plants. I've found that the best value is to use a hanging-basket-size container of impatiens with lots of blooms and buds to give your gift that full finished look. If hanging baskets aren't available, look for a large container with big, healthy impatiens.

alternative combination for sun

Here is a sun-loving arrangement of three plants to use as an alternative combination. Follow the same planting directions as described above.

(1) 1-gallon container of 'Angelface Blue' angelonia (*Angelonia augustifolia* hybrid)

(2) 1-quart containers of 'Intensia Lavender' phlox (*Phlox* hybrid)

(2) 6-inch pots of 'Blue Yonder' plectranthus (*Plectranthus* hybrid)

LEFT *From large to small, impatiens blooms come in a size that is the perfect fit. Super-sized varieties of New Guinea impatiens have flowers that are nearly twice the size of a standard impatiens, while mini varieties are truly tiny in comparison. Try small flowering impatiens as fillers in the front of the border. Plant a swath of standard impatiens in three slightly different shades to create a lively mass of color in a shady border.* **ABOVE** *The larger, bold blooms of New Guinea impatiens are particularly effective as a focal point in a container such as this one.*

flower, fruit, vegetable and herb window box

After Mother's Day, the weather begins to settle down and I look forward to filling my garden with more flowers, fruits, vegetables, and herbs. One early-spring day, I arrived at the garden center before the plants had been moved to their individual sections of the nursery, and as I looked over the ground where the fruits, vegetables, and herbs mingled so beautifully, an idea occurred to me. Rather than arrange these plants separately in a container, as we so often do, I thought it would be fun to try combining all three into a window-box design.

materials

Wooden window box, 24 inches long by 8 inches wide by 10 inches deep
Plastic garbage bag
(1) 16-quart bag of pottery soil
Small jar of water-retentive polymers
Small jar of slow-release fertilizer
Staple gun
Electric drill and drill bit
(2) 3-inch pots of Alaska Mix nasturtiums
(1) 6-pack of 'Red Sails' lettuce
(2) 3-inch pots of curly parsley (*Petroselinum crispum* 'Pagoda')
(2) 3-inch pots of flatleaf parsley
(2) 3-inch pots of bronze fennel (*Foeniculum vulgare* 'Rubrum')
(2) 3-inch pots of lemon-scented thyme (*Thymus*)
(1) 3-inch pot of pennyroyal (*Mentha pulegium*)
(3) 4-inch pots of 'Samba' geraniums
(2) 3-inch pots of 'Ozark Beauty' strawberries
(1) 3-inch pot of 'Oriental Limelight' artemisia

1. Line the wooden box with a garbage bag cut to fit the interior dimensions, securing it with staples along the insides of the box. Drill small holes through the bottom for drainage.

2. Fill the box two-thirds full with potting soil.

3. Mix in a small handful of water-retentive polymer crystals (follow label directions).

4. Add slow-release fertilizer (follow label directions).

5. Evenly space the geraniums along the back of the window box.

6. Add the other tall plants—the bronze fennel and 'Oriental Limelight' artemisia—along the back among the geraniums.

7. Now plant the remaining short and cascading plants toward the front and sides of the box.

8. Fill in between the plants with more soil, firmly pressing it in.

9. Water the box and mount it in a location in full sun.

care tips

There are a lot of plants in the box, so be sure to water daily. If you plan on harvesting the herbs, strawberries, and lettuce, use nontoxic forms of pest control. If the threat of a sudden cold snap is still possible where you live, you can move the box inside for the night.

SIGNATURE PLANT

1. 'Negrita'
2. 'Queen of the Night', 'Black Parrot', and 'Black Hero'
3. 'Lady Jane'
4. 'Perestroyka' and 'Temple of Beauty'
5. 'Portofino'
6. 'Princess Irene', 'Negrita', and 'Perestroyka'
7. 'Big Apricot'
8. 'Menton'
9. Sherbet Colorblends

Tulips

If you're the kind of person who loves a beautifully wrapped present, then tulips were made with you in mind. Like hidden treasures, these little prepackaged gifts from nature are all boxed up in neat brown wrappers that you plant in the fall and open in the spring. Every spring, it's a present I look forward to receiving. While some of my plantophile friends look down their noses at tulips and regard them as being too common, I love their over-the-top show quality and can't be without them. Their large chalice-shaped blooms appeal to both the gardener and the artist in me because they help me "paint" large areas with bold strokes of color.

I.
2.
3.
4.
5.
6.
7.
8.
9.

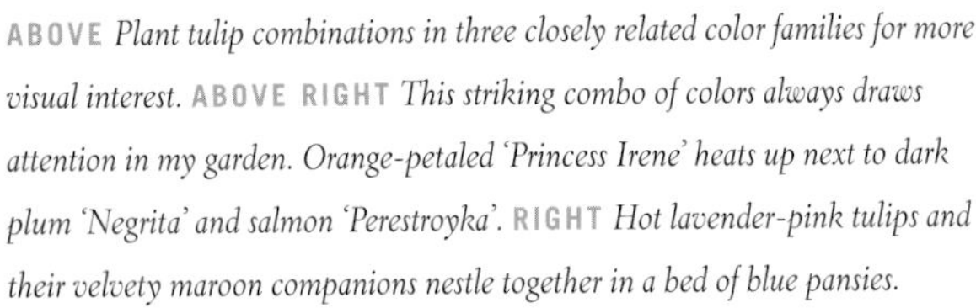

ABOVE *Plant tulip combinations in three closely related color families for more visual interest.* **ABOVE RIGHT** *This striking combo of colors always draws attention in my garden. Orange-petaled 'Princess Irene' heats up next to dark plum 'Negrita' and salmon 'Perestroyka'.* **RIGHT** *Hot lavender-pink tulips and their velvety maroon companions nestle together in a bed of blue pansies.*

Tulip Color Combinations

As the last of the late-season daffodils bloom, the tulips are making their big entrance. There's no doubt about it, when the tulips open their chalice-shaped cups, they have the full attention of any garden visitor. Since I plant early-, mid-, and late-season tulips, the show has already begun before Mother's Day, but by now, if the weather has been kind and cool, the full show is on.

When the tulips set my garden ablaze with their blooms, it's my chance not only to appreciate their beauty but also to evaluate my color choices. Sometimes I like to plant large drifts of the same variety of tulips, while other times I get the bug to experiment with different color combinations. Although I've had my share of failures, when I listen to my painter's heart the results are usually satisfying.

One lesson I've transferred from the easel to the garden is that colors look best when applied in large sweeps. Dots and dabs get lost and your eye tends to skip around to find unity in the design. So while a single tulip may indeed be an object of beauty, a large block, handsomely arranged, can be breathtaking. To make an impact, the minimum number of bulbs I plant together is 15 to 30. Even a small-scale garden can benefit from this approach. You can easily pack that many and more into a container or window box to create a burst of color.

One fall I planted a bed of tulip bulbs under my crabapple trees and mixed them with other spring bulbs and flowers. The next spring as the flowers came into bloom, I could see that it was one of my best efforts because I followed a few basic design rules. First, the tulips were what I call "color cousins," or closely related in the same color family. The collection ranged from shades of near white to pale pink and dark pink to salmon-pink. I chose that combination to play off of the blooms of the 'Narragansett' crabapple tree that flowered at the same time.

Another reason this design had impact was that I planted the bulbs in front of a boxwood hedge. The flower colors popped against that solid block of dark green. I also paid attention to the mature size of the tulips and planted the taller ones, in this case 'Menton', in the back and the shorter ones, 'Douglas Baader' and 'Elizabeth Arden', in the front. I finished out the display with a mix of blue violas, pansies, and dark muscari along the leading edge. The effect lasted a long time because I chose a mix of tulip varieties that had overlapping bloom times. Some flowered in early spring, others mid- and late spring, extending the bloom time over several months.

Since tulips are more of a here-today-gone-tomorrow kind of flower, I don't think of them as I do other mainstay garden plants. I love them for their shock value and throw them out there more as sensational, albeit temporary, garden embellishments. Place tulips where you can enjoy them the most and see them while they are in bloom. I love to catch a glimpse of them from a window inside the house, or along the path as I walk to the front door. They bloom happily in containers and window boxes, so position these portable gardens in locations where you won't miss the show. Use them as punctuation points around the garden. And be sure to plant enough so that you can cut big armfuls to bring inside.

COLOR COMBINATIONS	TULIP VARIETY
Orange-red	'Temple of Beauty'
Salmon	'Perestroyka'
Light salmon	'Menton'
Dark plum	'Negrita'
Purple	'Cum Laude'
Lavender	'Lilac Perfection'
Pink	'Queen of Bartigons'
Green	'Greenland'
Cream	'Maureen'
Yellow	'Cistula'
Green	'Spring Green'
Cream	'Maureen'
Blue	'Crown Azure Blue' pansy

fresh herbs at your finger tips

One of the many delights of spring is growing fresh herbs to add to recipes. Here's a fun way to have them close at hand. Adorn a wall, door, gate, or tabletop with a living ring of aromatic plants to create an attractive and fragrant accent to your garden home. This project elevates the stature of herbs from useful and hardworking garden plants to a decorative work of art that shows off the beauty of their colors and textures.

The secret to growing herbs on a wall is planting them in a living wreath form. The coated ring has front and back halves that either hook together or are fastened together with wire. Adjust the number of herbs you purchase to fill the ring based on the form's diameter.

materials

12-inch-diameter living wreath form
Floral wire (for non-hooking wreath forms)
Heavy scissors to cut wire (for non-hooking wreath forms)
Sheet moss, moistened
Pro-Mix container soil, moistened
Trailing or prostrate rosemary (*Rosmarinus officinalis* 'Prostratus')
(3) 3-inch pots of golden variegated sage (*Salvia officinalis* 'Icterina')
(3) 3-inch pots of oregano (*Origanum vulgare*)
(3) 3-inch pots of 'Lime' thyme (*Thymus x citriodorus* 'Lime')
(3) 3-inch pots of variegated lemon thyme (*Thymus x citriodorus* 'Variegata')

1. Place the bottom half of the wire wreath form flat on a table. This will be your container. Line the container half of the wreath form with damp sheet moss. Make sure to cover it well so there aren't any thin areas. Push down on the moss in the center to create a trough.

2. Fill the trough in the moss with soil and then place the top of the wreath form into position and hook or wire it to the bottom half.

3. Slip the plants out of their nursery pots and compress the roots by squeezing them in your hand. Work the plant roots into the moss and soil between the wires. Alternate the plant varieties around the wreath so their different colors and forms contrast with each other. For example, plant the golden variegated sage next to the trailing rosemary. Their foliage and leaf size are very different, so when they are combined, both stand out rather than blending with each other.

4. When all the plants are in place, add a little more soil and cover bare spots by poking a little moss between the wires.

5. Soak the wreath for a minute or so in a large saucer of water, and then lift it out and let it dry a bit so it isn't dripping. Hang it on a door or trellis or lay it flat as an accent on an outdoor table.

Herbs grow best in sunny locations, and although most can take a certain amount of dryness, be sure to check the soil regularly and keep the wreath watered. As the plants grow, tidy things up by trimming the plants with scissors. Don't forget to use the trimmings!

A fun alternative to an herb wreath is a selection of succulents, sedums and sempervivums, or even various types of ivy.

cut-flower garden

One of the benefits of having a flower garden is filling the house with vases of colorful, fragrant blooms. But often I find it's hard to cut large amounts of blooms from my flower borders without diminishing the look of the garden's display. My remedy is to create an out-of-the-way cutting garden where I can grow and gather as many flowers as I need to create the arrangements I use throughout my home.

materials

Shovel
Garden rake
Soil amendments
Scraps or strips of wood in 3-foot lengths
Packets of flower seeds
Flats of flower seedlings
Measuring tape
Wooden stakes
Hammer
Twine or string

1. Find a strip of ground in a sunny location about 3 feet wide and 12 feet long (the size may vary for your situation).

2. Prepare the seedbeds by removing the sod and turning over the soil to a depth of 18 inches and then add soil amendments such as compost, sand, and organic fertilizers as needed and rake until smooth.

3. Hammer a stake in the ground at the back corners of the bed. Tie a piece of twine to each stake to create a line that runs along the length of the bed. Measuring off that line, divide the bed into 3-foot sections, hammering a stake into the ground along the front of the bed every 3 feet. Lay the wooden strips on top of the ground as temporary guides to mark out each square.

4. Within each square plant packets of seeds or flats of nursery plants. If planting next to a fence, use the vertical surface to grow vining plants.

5. Keep the soil consistently moist.

continues on following pages

6. When seedlings are up, plants may need to be thinned. Plants grown as cut flowers can be spaced more closely than recommended, as this encourages long stems. For example, space zinnias 6 to 9 inches apart rather than 9 to 12.

Once your flowers bloom, follow these special tips as you collect, prepare, and arrange your bouquets.

For my seed selections, I choose varieties of flowers and foliage that grow quickly and have a long vase life:

- **'Soraya' sunflowers** (*Helianthus annuus* 'Soraya')—Rather than one flower per stem like many sunflowers, this beauty is loaded with lots of 6-inch blooms.
- **'Benary's Giant Bright Pink' zinnias** (*Zinnia elegans* 'Benary's Giant Bright Pink')—Cutting these colorful dahlia-like blossoms encourages the plant to grow more.
- **Polish amaranth** (*Amaranthus cruentus*)—The dark wine foliage can be cut for bouquets even before the plant's upright burgundy chenille-like flowers bloom.
- **Green love-lies-bleeding** (*Amaranthus caudatus* 'Viridis')—The unusual cascading, chenille-like flowers offer great form, texture, and color foils in bouquets. The flowers also dry well for fall arrangements.
- **'Benary's Giant Lime' zinnias** (*Zinnia elegans* 'Benary's Giant Lime')—The large, round, light green blooms freshen a bouquet.
- **'Molten Lava' amaranth** (*Amaranthus tricolor* 'Molten Lava')—Its flamboyant foliage adds zest to any floral display.
- **Hyacinth bean vine** (*Dolichos lablab*)—Add luxurious lengths of this vine for its lilac blossoms and shiny magenta seedpods.
- **'Flamingo Purple' celosia** (*Celosia spicata* 'Flamingo Purple')—This adds drama with its dark purple foliage and dark pink wheatlike flower spikes.
- **'Benary's Giant Orange' zinnias** (*Zinnia elegans* 'Benary's Giant Orange')—This cultivar offers big and bright orange flowers.
- **'Bicolor Rose' gomphrena** (*Gomphrena globosa* 'Bicolor Rose')—Loads of these nickel-sized ball-shaped blooms look great clustered in arrangements.

gather the flowers

- Cut in early morning, when flowers are fresh.
- Bring along sharp clippers and a container of water.
- Choose blossoms that are newly opened and buds that are just beginning to unfurl.
- Cut stems a few inches longer than you'll need in the vase.
- Make clean cuts that don't crush the flower stems.
- Cut flowers one at a time and immediately place them in water.

ready the blooms

- Remove all leaves that will be underwater in the vase (left on, they breed bacteria).
- Fill a deep nonmetal container with warm (not hot) water.
- Under running water, recut an inch or two from each stem on a slant (this increases the surface area for the flower to take up water).
- Place directly into the container of warm water.
- Put the container in a cool, dark spot for at least 2 hours.

set up the vase

- Choose a vase that complements the bouquet in size, shape, and color.
- Look for fun, out-of-the ordinary containers such as jugs, pitchers, pretty bottles—even fruit or vegetable cans with great-looking labels. Check out import aisles at the supermarket or specialty food stores.
- If the container is large or won't hold water, conceal a cup or jar inside for the flowers.
- Fill with water and add a packet of flower food (one packet per quart), available at florist or craft stores. If you run out of prepackaged floral preservative, try a homemade recipe of lemon-lime soda (not diet) at the rate of 2 parts water to 1 part soda. Add ¼ teaspoon of bleach per quart to inhibit bacteria.

arranging the flowers

- Before putting the flowers in the vase, gather them in your hand.
- Start with a few stems at a time.
- Hold them at arm's length to see how they fit together.
- Gently pull from the top if a flower is out of place.
- Once you're satisfied, use your free hand to cut the stems the same length.
- Place them in the vase and loosen the cluster to fill the container.
- Add more flowers if needed.

Peonies

It's hard to believe that spring is drawing to a close. Not only do the plants that have come and gone tell me so, but also increasingly warmer days have arrived, hinting that summer's hot, lazy days lie just ahead. But happily, before the season bows out, spring leaves me with a final encore performance that is as thrilling as any of the earlier acts. One plant, the peony, will bring the house to its feet during the closing moments of the season.

In the plant world, peonies rank at the top of the list, prized for their form, stunning range of colors, and exceptional hardiness. Few other plants once established bloom so reliably year after year with such little care. Their large, round flowers add bright pops of color against their rounded mounds of dark foliage. And their intoxicating fragrance makes them a wonderful cut flower. Peonies are a great value, providing years of beautiful returns.

Now, that's not to say they have no downside. To be robust, the plants require a certain number of cooling days in the winter. My Zone 7 garden sits on the edge of the divide between all the varieties I want to grow and those that do best in southern gardens. Plant breeders have come to the rescue with new and better cultivars that can take the heat, solving one of my dilemmas. They are also helping me with another challenge: The varieties I seem to gravitate toward are the saucer-sized multipetaled blooms that are heavy headed. After one good rain, the blooms fill up with water and I find them flattened on the ground, forlorn and spattered with mud. New varieties are being developed with stronger stems to keep the flowers aloft.

Mid-May to early June is prime time to enjoy these splendid flowers. There are two types of peonies grown in the home landscape: the garden or herbaceous peony, which grows 2 to 3 feet tall and dies back in the fall, and the tree peony, which is 4 to 6 feet in height and produces a woody stem that does not die back to the ground in the winter.

Although autumn is the time to plant peonies, now is the time to pick your favorites, so you can select the right color and variety for your garden. Visit display gardens and take a picture or record the names of the ones you like best. Check local nursery centers in your area to see which varieties are best suited for your garden.

You can place an order with a mail-order company this spring and they will ship the tubers in the fall when the time is right to plant them in your area. You can also wait and buy plants this fall from your local garden center.

Warm-Blooded Beauties

If you live in the Deep South or other areas with warm summers and mild winters, keep in mind that peonies need cool temperatures to really thrive. Most varieties require night temperatures of 40 degrees F or lower for at least 6 weeks a year. But I always love to defy the naysayers who insist "you can't grow that here!" So when I designed a garden in southwest Georgia, I convinced the family to plant two varieties I've had much success with: 'Festiva Maxima' and 'Sarah Bernhardt'. To my critics' amazement—and envy, I might add—the peonies bloomed profusely.

Southern gardeners should consider early- to midseason-blooming cultivars, such as 'Kansas', 'Miss America', 'Big Ben', and 'Red Charm'. Later-flowering varieties have a tendency to develop weaker stems and although they produce flower buds, the warm weather usually keeps them from opening properly. Single- or Japanese-form flowers are also good bets. Another tip is to plant peonies where they will get afternoon shade.

LEFT *Deep red blooms of 'Douglas Brand' peonies mix beautifully with 'New Dawn' rose, 'Camelot' foxgloves, artemisia 'Powis Castle', and the starburst blooms of* Allium schubertii. BELOW LEFT *Single varieties such as these 'Sarah Bernhardt' peonies make stunning presentations all by themselves.* BELOW RIGHT *'Sarah Bernhardt' and ' Festiva Maxima' peonies displayed in French watering cans add a luxurious welcome to an outdoor setting.*

WHAT ABOUT THE ANTS?

If you grow peonies, you may have noticed that ants are attracted to the sweet sap produced by the peony bud. This is no cause for alarm. The ants are not harmful. Just leave them alone, and once the flowers bloom, they'll move on. Or, they can be easily washed off if you cut the blooms for indoor bouquets.

Coming to Terms

As you look through catalogs to choose peonies for your garden, you'll find that herbaceous peonies are classified by their blooming time and flower form. Some look like hefty corsages, while others are light and delicate. Depending on the variety, the flower may be bowl, saucer, or cup shaped. Here are a few of the terms used to describe their blooms.

- SINGLE: five or more petals in a single layer around pollen-bearing stamens.
- SEMIDOUBLE: similar to the single form but with several layers of petals around pollen-bearing center stamens.
- JAPANESE: single or semidouble petals around showy stamens that resemble petals; also known as anemone.
- BOMB DOUBLE: many petals with a rounded center.
- DOUBLE: large petal-packed blooms and no visible stamens.

Simply Sumptuous Blossoms

Here is just a sampling of the hundreds of peony varieties available.

'AURORA SUNRISE' The bright pink Japanese-style flower of this peony is highlighted with a tightly packed golden center. A 30-inch variety, it was developed for good stem strength and a striking presence in the garden. Zones 2–8.

'CORAL SUPREME' This gorgeous, 36-inch semidouble peony has stunning salmon-coral, cup-shaped blossoms that open early in the season. Zones 2–8.

'FESTIVA MAXIMA' Developed in 1851, this fragrant, early-blooming, 24- to 30-inch peony is an old-fashioned favorite. Strong stems provide good support for the large white, double flowers with crimson markings. Zones 4–8.

'GARDENIA' Large (8- to 10-inch) blush-white gardenia-shaped flowers bloom on strong 34-inch-long stems. This is an early- to midseason bloomer with a sweet fragrance. Zones 3–8.

'HESPERUS' A tree peony (3 to 5 feet), this blooms in midseason with single dusty rose flowers with yellow undertones and deep rose veins. The flowers sport crinkled petals that are notched with purple inner flares and fine, golden stamens. Zones 4–8.

'HIGHLIGHT' This peony helps extend your flower show by blooming midseason with large, dark red double flowers. A beautiful cut flower growing to 34 inches, its rich color adds depth and drama to a bed or border. Zones 3–8.

'PETTICOAT FLOUNCE' This peony lives up to its name with superb soft pink "bomb"-shaped blossoms touched in creamy white and edged with tinges of red. An excellent cut flower with luxurious, deep green foliage growing to 24 inches, it blooms early in the season. Zones 2–8.

'RED EMPEROR' Very large, Japanese-type bright red flowers with full pale centers make a striking display as they bloom in midseason. The intense color fades, which only makes this showy flower even more interesting. Grows to 30 inches. Zones 3–8.

'REINE HORTENSE' Another old-fashioned beauty introduced in 1857, this fragrant peony features large, double flowers that bloom in midseason. Flowers are rose-pink in color and have fluffy petals that are notched and silvered at the tips. The plant's strong stems and deep green foliage make it a standout in the flower border. Zones 3–8.

'SARAH BERNHARDT' More than a century has passed since this peony was introduced in 1906, but it is still a popular favorite. A double flower in dark rose-pink with petals edged in a slightly lighter color makes this fragrant, mid- to late-season bloomer the star attraction. Zones 3–8.

'SEA SHELL' One of the best peonies for the South, this Gold Medal Winner is the center of attraction in any garden. The lively pink single flower has a bright center of yellow stamens. Flowering in midseason, this 36-inch peony holds its blooms high on strong stems. Zones 3–8.

OPPOSITE, CLOCKWISE FROM TOP RIGHT *'Krinkled White' peony, a heat-tolerant variety, was introduced over seventy years ago and is still unmatched in beauty; 6-inch white blossoms with showy golden yellow stamens open in early May. A show-stopper in any border, 'Douglas Brand' has 9- to 10-inch watermelon-red double flowers. The show is about to begin in this bed of soon-to-be-blooming 'Mrs. Franklin D. Roosevelt' peonies. Early-blooming 'Miss America' peony bears snow-white semi-double flowers with a yellow center.*

Peony Presentations

Peonies make superb cut flowers, especially the single and Japanese forms. When putting together a vase arrangement, I harvest the flowers as early in the morning as possible when they are fresh and fully hydrated. If they are covered in dew, gently shake them to remove the water. Choose stems that are 18 inches long, and leave at least two leaves on the stem that remains on the plant. It's a good idea not to cut more than half of the flowers from a single plant, since that would remove too much of the plant's foliage.

If you want to use the flowers in an arrangement immediately, choose blooms that are almost fully open. I've found that a bouquet of peonies lasts longer if I select flowers that are in various stages of opening. Professional growers harvest peonies only in bud stage, just as the buds start to soften and when they are barely showing any color. This ensures that they have time to get the flowers to market before the buds open.

When I arrange peonies, I like to add a generous amount of foliage. The combination looks more natural and reflects the look of the entire plant. Remember to remove foliage that falls below the waterline, and display the arrangement in areas away from heat and direct sunlight.

Fixing the Flops

Some people avoid planting peonies because the flowers tend to flop on the ground after a heavy rain. If you are starting with new plants, look for varieties that are described as having strong stems, such as 'Charlie's White' or 'Angel Cheeks', the latter a pink bomb double. Furthermore, flowers that are classified as single, Japanese, or semidouble have fewer petals, so they don't hold as much rainwater as the double-petaled varieties.

If you already have a plant in your garden that is a "flopper," pick some of the blooms for indoor arrangements before they fully open. That way, you can enjoy the flowers indoors before they succumb to a storm.

Finally, you can support your peonies by staking them as they grow. Look for grow-through supports (round wire grids atop three stakes) and place this support over the top of your peonies when new shoots emerge in early spring. As the peonies get taller, the shoots will grow through the openings of the grid and eventually conceal the structure.

You can also make a homemade version of this system by surrounding your peonies with any type of stake, stringing garden twine around the stakes, and then crisscrossing the twine between the stakes to form a grid.

LEFT *Bamboo stakes and twine are all you need to make a low-tech support for heavy-blossomed peonies. Be sure to drive the stakes into the ground a few inches so they won't pull out. You may prefer to use dark green gardener's twine so the support is less apparent.* OPPOSITE, LEFT *The soft seashell-pink petals of 'Mrs. Franklin D. Roosevelt' peony unfold one layer at a time and the stems have several side buds that prolong the plant's bloom time.* OPPOSITE, RIGHT *Every year I look forward to creating a sumptuous arrangement with 'Bowl of Beauty' blossoms. The flower's frilly center is ringed with soft lavender outer petals.*

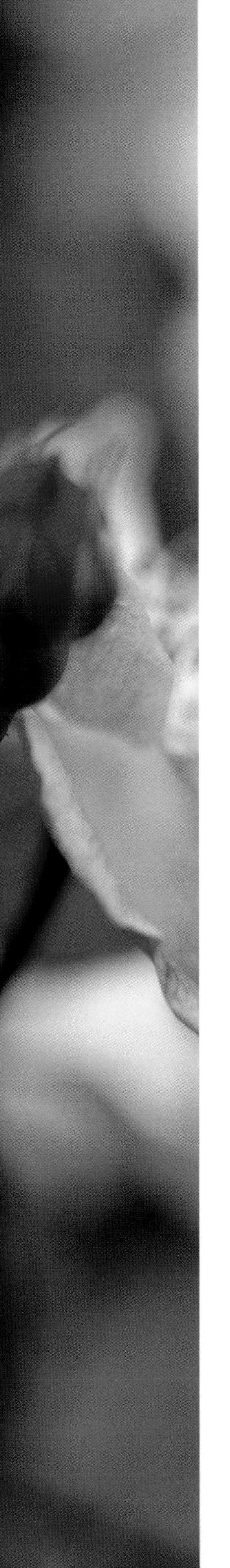

summer.

Summer's stage has many moods and several set changes. The first act opens with a cast of peonies, roses, larkspur, and irises. The duration of each plant's performance is under the direction of the weather. If temperatures soar quickly, petals can open and fall in just a few days. But if nature is kind, there are long, cool spells allowing ample time to enjoy the presentation. Deciduous trees and shrubs, decked out in full costume, cast dark pockets of cool shade about them. Spring's youthful exuberance has nearly run its course, and a calmer, more mature garden in deeper tones of green materializes. A host of perennials that have patiently waited their turn in the footlights set buds in anticipation of their cameo. A pageantry of plants is set in motion and I'm delighted to be engaged in the spectacle.

As the summer sun arcs higher in the sky, my garden responds, elevating leaf and bloom toward the light. Very soon, my roses will open—an event that marks the time when spring takes its final bow—and I know that summer has truly arrived. From that moment on I take special delight as the garden unfolds in all its seasonal finery; soon my hydrangeas will be in peak bloom, and my borders will be filled with the sweet perfume of garden lilies.

These are the days that I longed for in winter; I can kick off my shoes and go barefoot in the grass, enjoy the taste of my first homegrown tomato, and fill the table with fresh-cut flowers. Things seem less urgent now: It's time to slow down and have more parties. A way I like to share the beauty of my summer garden is to invite friends and their children over for an afternoon of playing in the dirt. Kids personalize their own buckets and then fill them with soil and plants. Throwing a container party is a great way to give children their first hands-on experience in the garden.

As the summer sets in and temperatures climb, my front porch and loggia become shady retreats. They are also great settings for dining alfresco and enjoying the cooler twilight hours. I like to make them inviting places where friends want to linger, with lots of comfortable furnishings, colorful containers, and beautiful accessories.

Since most of the planting was done in the spring, maintenance mode sets in. After weeding and watering the garden, my creative efforts turn to put together several simple projects like a rustic rose trellis, string vine supports, and an ivy topiary. These activities are enjoyable ways to enhance the look of my garden as it grows and matures through the summer.

At the first sign of cooler temperatures, the "waste not–want not" side of my personality kicks in and I gather up as many garden goodies as I can to either savor now or keep for another day. Before the cold takes my first summer rose, I cut armloads of flowers to enjoy as fresh bouquets or preserve as dried flowers for autumn displays.

CLOCKWISE FROM TOP RIGHT *Colorful bouquets of mixed blooms convey the abundance of summer and add a lively touch to the table. A window box brims with 'Infinity Dark Pink' New Guinea impatiens, 'Jellybean Rose' impatiens, 'Fishnet Stockings' coleus, and trailing 'Goldilocks' lysimachia. Containers of 'Evergold' carex, 'Jellybean Cherry Rose' impatiens, 'Dolce Key Lime' heuchera, and 'Charmed Wine' oxalis complement the arrangement. The local farmer's market offers fresh produce for a weekend meal. Watering the garden gives me a chance to slow down and look carefully at each plant so I can better appreciate its beauty and growth.*

A Rose for Every Garden

Over the years, I have managed to squeeze in more than thirty different varieties of roses into my urban-sized garden. They are so versatile in the landscape that I can always find a rose that's perfectly suited to cover an arbor, star in a mixed flower border, or fill a container. So when people tell me that they don't have the right conditions to grow roses, I always say, "Oh, but you do!"

I've listed below rose varieties that address the most common concerns gardeners have about growing roses, and you can always find additional advice for growing roses in your area from local nurseries. If you haven't already fallen under their wonderful spell, I hope one of these selections will inspire you to add a rose to your garden.

ROSES RESISTANT TO BLACK SPOT

'Caldwell Pink'
'Katharina Zeimet'
'Lamarque'
'Marchesa Boccella'
'Marie Pavié'
'New Dawn'
'Pinkie'
'Russell's Cottage'
'The Fairy'
'White Dawn'

Easy-Care Roses

'BELINDA'S DREAM' Large, free-flowering roses are produced on an upright shrub throughout the growing season. These plants have all the beauty of a hybrid tea with none of the worry. Shrub, 1992; 3 to 6 feet; Zones 5–9; fragrant, pink blooms.

'MARIE PAVIE' A very versatile variety, it blooms continuously throughout the season. Sweet fragrance and nearly thornless canes make it one of my favorites to enjoy indoors as a cut flower. Polyantha, 1888; 3 to 4 feet; Zones 5–9; fragrant, white blooms.

'NEWN' This rose is the most untroubled rose that I grow. Pale pink blooms appear all summer. Climber, 1930; 12 to 20 feet; Zones 5–9; fragrant, pale pink blooms maturing to cream.

'OLD BLUSH' I grow 'Old Blush' along my picket fence next to a burgundy barberry and purple iris. It is a heavy bloomer that requires little attention. In the fall it produces a nice display of rose hips. China, 1752; 3 to 6 feet; Zones 6–9; fragrant, medium pink blooms.

Roses That Tolerate Light Shade

'BUFF BEAUTY' I love apricot roses and this is one of the best. The medium-size, fully double blooms borne in clusters perfume the air on warm days. Foliage is vigorous, spreading, and dark green. This variety is hardy in poor soil and will bloom with a half day of shade or dappled light. Musk, 1939; 5 to 7 feet; Zones 6–9; fragrant, apricot blooms.

'GRUSS AN AACHEN' This is a favorite for lightly shaded areas. The large blooms appear repeatedly over the summer. Floribunda, 1909; 3 to 4 feet; Zones 6–9; fragrant, pink blooms with hints of yellow.

'LAMARQUE' I have trained this rose over the door to my chicken house. It receives morning sun but is shaded in the afternoon, and yet it blooms profusely sometimes well into December. Noisette, 1830; 12 to 20 feet; Zones 7–9; fragrant, pale cream blooms.

'MME. ALFRED CARRIERE' This rose is a vigorous climber with showy, super-fragrant blooms. In my garden it grows up through a holly hedge into the limbs of a 'Byers White' crape myrtle. Even in that partially shaded setting, it blooms. Noisette, 1879; 15 to 20 feet; Zones 6–9; fragrant, pale pink blooms maturing to white.

Roses for Cold Climates

'ALCHYMIST' This rose covers itself with apricot-gold flowers. Although it blooms only once a season, its carefree nature makes it worth growing. Shrub, 1956; 10 to 12 feet; Zones 4–9; fragrant, once-blooming, apricot blooms.

'CAREFREE WONDER' Large 4-inch blooms grace a compact shrub all season long. This variety is very adaptable to a range of growing conditions and produces nice large orange hips in the fall. Shrub, 1990; 3 to 4 feet; Zones 4–9; medium pink blooms with a white eye.

'FANTIN-LATOUR' Although the blooms suggest the classic cabbage rose, the origins of 'Fantin-Latour' are a mystery. Flat, multipetaled pink blooms appear amid dark green foliage. The canes are nearly thornless, making this a favorite cut flower. Centifolia (cabbage rose), unknown date of origin; 4 to 6 feet; Zones 4–9; fragrant, once-blooming, light pink flowers.

'MME PLANTIER' This attractive rose is planted at the corner of my front porch by the steps. Covered in clusters of white, fragrant blooms it offers a sweet welcome. Alba, 1835; 4 to 6 feet; Zones 4–9; fragrant, once-blooming, white blooms.

'THE FAIRY' Plant this rose among annuals and perennials for a lovely mixed border. 'The Fairy' has a lush, spreading shape that will soften any angle. The small, bright green, shiny leaves and the clustered sprays of petite, double pink roses are on display throughout the growing season. Summer sun fades the flowers to blush white, adding to their charm. Polyantha, 1932; 3 to 4 feet; Zones 4–9; light pink blooms.

ABOVE *Fragrant pink blooms and old-fashioned charm make David Austin's English 'Cottage Rose' ideal for a small garden.* **BELOW** *Although a modern rose, 'Alchymist' is reminiscent of an old rose with its intricate quartered blooms.* **OPPOSITE, LEFT** *'LaMarne' is a wonderful landscape rose that's virtually carefree; it's not bothered by blackspot or powdery mildew, and it blooms well with only morning sun.* **OPPOSITE, RIGHT** *'Nearly Wild' is a neat and compact plant that is perfect as a low hedge or in a container.*

Roses for Small Spaces

'CALDELL PINK' This rose will reward you with nonstop pink flowers on a compact shrub. It requires little maintenance and will thrive in just about any soil. Polyantha, date of origin unknown; 3 to 4 feet; Zones 6–9; medium pink blooms.

'CÉCILE BRUNNER' Here is a rose that never lets me down. It produces a treasure box of miniature hybrid tea–shaped blooms all summer long. I never have to spray it for black spot or insects and it thrives in partial shade. Polyantha, 1881; 3 to 4 feet; Zones 5–9; fragrant, light pink blooms.

'CLOTILDE SOUPERT' 'Clotilde Soupert' produces miniature cabbagelike blooms that are a pale cream. I find it to be a nice addition to the flower border and for containers. The fragrance is pleasant and the plant is fairly carefree. Polyantha, 1890; 3 to 4 feet; Zones 6–9; fragrant, white blooms.

'WHITE PET' As the name implies, this is a darling of a rose. Fully double, white roses adorn this diminutive shrub. It is perfect for containers or other tight spaces where you want to add blooms and fragrance. Polyantha, 1879; 2 to 3 feet; Zones 5–9; fragrant, white blooms.

ABOVE *Climber 'New Dawn' rose, with its lush dark green foliage and abundant clusters of sweetly fragrant, 3- to 4-inch, pearl-blush flowers, has long been a favorite of mine.* **RIGHT** *Draped over a stone wall, 'New Dawn' adds a romantic, charming quality to the garden.* **OPPOSITE** *Dating from 1752, 'Old Blush' has parented some of the great rose classics, and remains one of the most popular roses on its own merits.*

Rx for Roses

I don't want to mislead you. All roses require a little hand-holding, although to be sure some are more self-sufficient than others. Here's a routine that I follow to keep my roses in tiptop shape.

FEEDING. Early in the spring, I give my roses a healthy dose of fertilizer to fortify them for their first flush of bloom. I use a fertilizer high in phosphorus (5-10-5), which is the middle number on the package. After the first wave of flowers fades, if the roses are repeat bloomers, I hit them with a second application of 5-10-5 fertilizer. This will reenergize the plants and promote more blooms. Through the summer I continue to feed my repeat-blooming roses after each flower cycle. I also use organic rose fertilizers that supply nutrients to the rose and help improve the quality of the soil by contributing organic matter.

BLACK SPOT AND POWDERY MILDEW. One of the most common complaints about growing roses is dealing with black spot and powdery mildew, particularly in areas of the country where summers are humid. Black spot, as the name implies, starts with a black spot on the leaf. It's a fungus that certainly diminishes the look of the plant. I've never had a rosebush actually die from black spot, but it can certainly cut down on the shrubs' performance and make them look pretty shabby.

HOME REMEDY

Some people have found this formula useful as a preventive to powdery mildew:

1 heaping teaspoon of baking soda
1 tablespoon of dormant oil
½ teaspoon of insecticidal soap or dishwashing soap
1 gallon of water

The dormant oil and insecticidal soap are available at garden centers. Be sure the plant is well hydrated before applying this solution. Water deeply a couple of days before spraying and avoid applying during the heat of the day.

Sometimes an application of a fungicide may be necessary. There are various products available to treat powdery mildew. I use a sulfur-based product or neem oil and spray about every 7 to 10 days when mildew is a problem.

Black spot is usually brought on by weather conditions. Sporadic rains followed by humid to hot conditions create the ideal breeding ground for this fungus. The rain soaks the plant, and then the hotter weather causes the fungus to form on the damp leaves and petals. If it becomes a real problem, you may choose to remove the rose and try other varieties bred to be more black-spot resistant. The problem cycles in and out of my garden, and by and large I just learn to live with it and not expect my roses to be without blemishes. There are commercial fungicides available, but they work best before the problem begins, not after you have a full-blown case. If you use a fungicide, always try to get the plant completely saturated from top to bottom with the spray. And you need to keep at it. Be sure to follow label directions. You should also spray the ground around your roses and put any diseased leaves in the trash, not in your compost pile.

Powdery mildew is another fungus that reveals itself as a powderlike coating over the leaves. It will rarely kill a plant, but a heavy infestation of powdery mildew causes a plant to lose its leaves, diminishing its vigor and affecting its capacity to flower.

If you're having this problem in your garden, there are some things you can do. Your first line of defense is prevention, so make sure you've given your plants plenty of room to breathe. If you do find your plants covered with this fungus, remove and dispose of infected plants and leaves. Don't put infected leaves in your compost pile, because that will just harbor spores for another round next season.

PRUNING AND DEADHEADING. The time to do any hard pruning of roses is in the late winter or early spring before the leaf buds open. Check out my advice on how to prune a rose at that time of the year on page 203. But don't panic if you didn't get around to cutting back your plants this year. Once the blooms have faded you will have the opportunity to do some light pruning. This will be the time to reshape and clean up your plants. Also, for the roses that are repeat bloomers, it will encourage a second round of flower production. It's important to realize that not all roses rebloom. Some old-fashioned shrub types bloom only once, in the spring. Cutting the spent flowers away on these types will just help the plant look a little better. But for those that rebloom, like my favorite 'New Dawn' as well as any of the floribundas, polyanthas, and popular hybrid tea roses, removing what is left of dead flowers will definitely encourage the next wave of bloom.

When you do this, it's crucial to clip them with sharp pruners, making the cut at a 45-degree angle just above a leaf with five leaflets. By cutting here, where the new bud forms, you ensure that the stem will be thick enough and strong enough to support it. I also prune the branches to keep the center of the plants open, which encourages air circulation and gives the plants a pleasing shape. Good air circulation helps deter fungal problems. You can also dictate the shape of your rose by the angle of your pruning cut; a cut angled into—or facing—the center of the plant will direct growth inward, while a cut angled toward the outside of the stem—facing away from the center of the plant—will ensure that your plant grows upward and outward. After I've pruned my roses, I feed them with a high-phosphorus liquid fertilizer (5-10-5) to encourage flowering.

ABOVE AND LEFT *'Russell's Cottage' rose blooms only once a season, but its blanket of fragrant flowers makes it all worthwhile. A closer look at this rose allows you to appreciate its richly hued blooms, which open crimson and then fade to a deep magenta.* **OPPOSITE** *A cloud of sweetly scented 'White Dawn' roses is held aloft on a metal trellis in my parterre garden.*

1. 'Abraham Darby'
2. 'Katherina Zeimet'
3. 'Madame Isaac Pierre'
4. 'Madame Alfred Carriere'
5. 'Climbing Iceberg' standard, 'Frau Karl Druschi' on arbor
6. 'Alba Meidiland'
7. 'Lamarque'
8. 'Scentimental'
9. 'Colette'

Roses

Okay, I'll admit it; I'm a complete nut about roses. This happy affliction began when I was a student in garden history and design in Manchester, England. As I toured the country's grand gardens, I fell under the spell of roses, particularly the heritage or heirloom varieties (those developed before 1867) and their entrancing qualities. Endowed with impressive pedigrees and stunning good looks, these classic beauties have been grown and treasured in European gardens for centuries. Upon my return to the United States, I found that very few people on this side of the pond were familiar with them. So, with great enthusiasm, I started incorporating them in my garden designs. Clients soon became converts and fell in love with their intoxicating fragrance, beautiful form, and ease of care. They were surprised and happy to discover that these heritage varieties were often more carefree and adaptable than hybrid tea roses.

1.
2.
3.
4.
5.
6.
7.
8.
9.

Rose Reinforcements

One way to show off your climbing roses and promote their growth is to provide supports to the canes as they grow. Adding a garden structure doesn't always have to be expensive or complicated. During my tours of English gardens, one of the things I found so charming was the use of twigs and branches to build simple garden features. These rustic structures create an Old World look that adds character to the youngest of gardens, and roses look terrific in contrast with the wooden framework. I also appreciate how rustic components blend well with several house styles. I've seen them used effectively in gardens with Colonial, Mediterranean, Victorian, or Greek Revival–style homes, not to mention a log cabin!

Here's a simple twig trellis, designed to be used in a container, that is a perfect support for a climbing rose or annual vine. It is so easy to do that you can put one together in an afternoon.

materials for rustic trellis

Tree limbs approximately 2 to 3 inches in diameter:
- 2 limbs 5 feet long
- 2 limbs 20 inches long
- 3 limbs 4 feet long

Hatchet or pruning saw
(1) box 10-penny galvanized nails
(1) roll 12-gauge copper wire
Electric drill
Hammer

materials for container

20- to 22-inch terra-cotta pot (I use a bell-shaped container)
Rustic trellis made of branches and copper wire
(1) 2- or 3-gallon 'Sugar Candy' clematis
(1) 2- or 3-gallon 'New Dawn' rose
(6) 1-quart pots of pink petunias
(2) 16-quart bags of potting soil
(1) small container of slow-release fertilizer
(1) small container of water-retentive polymers
(1) roll of garden twine
Pruners
Pruning saw
Leather gloves

1. Select and cut tree limbs of the appropriate length and diameter in the materials list. I use cedar limbs, but any sturdy wood is suitable. (If you don't have limbs available, bamboo is a great substitute, available at many garden centers.) The 5-foot limbs will serve as the vertical supports, the 20-inch branches will be the horizontal braces, and the 4-foot limbs will form the "X" pattern between the braces.

continues on following pages

2. Using hand pruners, remove small twigs and debris from the limbs. Shape the ends of the supports into points using a hatchet or pruning saw.

3. Lay out the two 5-foot limbs on the ground parallel to one another and 15 inches apart. Position one of the 4-foot limbs parallel in between these two. Measure down 8 inches from the top and place one of the 20-inch limbs across both of the longer limbs to form the top brace.

4. Place the bottom horizontal brace across the two vertical supports 28 inches from the top brace.

5. Position the remaining two 4-foot limbs between the horizontal braces to create an "X" pattern.

6. Using an electric drill with a ¼-inch bit, predrill holes for the nails where each joint meets.

7. Drive nails through the holes.

8. Wrap the joints of the rose support together with 12-gauge copper wire or other sturdy wire.

planting the container

Now you can plant your container with roses or a combination of roses and other companionable plants. Gardening for me is more than the appreciation of an individual flower. I really get excited about putting together great combinations of flowers such as clematis and roses, which complement each other so well. The thing you want to remember when matching them up is that they look best when there is enough color contrast between the two so you can appreciate the beauty of both. Clematis prefer growing conditions where their "feet" (roots) are in the shade and their faces are up in the sun, and the rose provides a perfect canopy for this. It is a classic combination.

To accomplish this design, fill the container almost to the rim with soil. Check the ingredients list on the bagged soil mix. If it doesn't have slow-release fertilizer and water-absorbing crystals, add those into the mix following label directions. Push the legs of the trellis down into the soil until it is stable. Plant the clematis so it is positioned slightly behind the trellis. Weave the vines into the trellis and secure them with pieces of twine or light string. Next, plant the rose in front of the trellis. Tie the rose branches into the supports to help train them in the right direction. Prune away any spindly or awkward-looking branches. Finish the project by planting pink petunias around the container's edge. Now, that's a picture.

Creating Comfort Zones

As summer sets in, I enjoy spending more time outside in the garden. When it's time to take a break, there are two spots that make great places to put my feet up and catch a cool breeze. One is a wraparound porch just outside my front door, and the other is my loggia, which is a covered walkway between the back door and garage. These areas are treated as indoor/outdoor rooms where I blend the comfort and style of my home's interior with the beauty of my garden. As fresh-air rooms decorated with elements of both worlds, they serve as seamless transitions between indoors and out and become extensions of my home's living space—places to relax, entertain, dine alfresco, read a book, or just watch the world go by. Here are some of the guidelines I use to create outdoor rooms with indoor comfort.

DEFINE THE SPOT. When you are looking around the outside of your house for a place to call your own, think about where you'd like to sit, rather than the size of the area. Even a postage-stamp-size spot can be transformed into an inviting setting. All it takes is room enough for a chair and a side table.

KEEP IT IN STYLE. As you begin to select furnishings, follow the style of your home's decor and architecture to guide your choices of colors, furniture, accessories, and plant. Try to echo elements from your home's interior style. I've found this method particularly important if you can see the outdoor setting from the interior of the home. When similar colors, patterns, and furniture style are used indoors and out, they blend together and enlarge the sense of space in both areas. Try to break the "white plastic chair syndrome" by finding outdoor furniture that serves as a better reflection of your

home's character. Garage sales, antiques stores, and home improvement centers offer a wide variety of options.

The same design considerations hold true when selecting plants. Choose plants that reflect your home's era and style. Roses suggest a casual cottage look, blousy ferns convey Victorian charm, cypress and bamboo impart Asian serenity, and cacti and succulents recall a Southwestern style. Your choice of containers is another opportunity to continue your home's theme outdoors.

PICK A PALETTE. When choosing colors for your setting, the basic rules apply: Vibrant reds, oranges, and yellows draw the eye, while cooler hues such as soft blues, pinks, and purples enlarge the sense of space. So as you think about developing a color scheme, consider if you want to make your setting look larger or smaller. Although my loggia isn't very wide, by using colors from the cooler side of the color wheel, I can make it feel more expansive. That's not to say that a bright pop of yellow or red isn't allowed. The key thing is that you find the colors appealing and that they convey the sense of restfulness or vibrancy that speaks to the kinds of activities you have planned for the room. You may want your entertainment spots to be festive and lively, but not the areas for reading or meditating. The colors you choose can help you express that feeling.

Various pieces of furniture in bright colors are best placed where you want to make a deliberate statement, such as eye-catching red chairs against a dark green hedge. In a muted green, the same set will blend in with their surroundings. In general, strongly patterned fabrics often look best near the house, especially if they carry a theme from indoors.

FEATURE A FOCAL POINT. Next time you walk into a new setting, try this little experiment. Notice the first place that draws your attention. Just like an interior room, an outdoor setting looks best when it is organized around a center of interest. In the absence of that, our eyes typically dart about the area until they can find somewhere to land. Use a hanging basket, a large houseplant, a planter, wall art, an outdoor fireplace, or a statue to create a focal point. And once you give your room that feature, make it easy for seated guests to see it by arranging furniture accordingly.

BLUR THE LINE. I've found that one of the best ways to give an outdoor seating arrangement plenty of indoor charm is to incorporate several "fool-the-eye" interior elements such as rugs, cushions, and other interior accessories. I love to include surprising touches such as a floor lamp, unbreakable chandelier, even a clock to give it that family-room feel. Today's weather-resistant fabrics and finishes make it easy to add color and pattern to a garden setting. Pile on the pillows, reupholster cushions, hang curtains, and dress up tables with vibrant weather-resistant fabrics. Gone are the days when all the fabric choices looked like window awnings. Now you can find fun, brightly-hued patterns that are beautiful and durable. I know some people who love the fabrics so much that they are using them both indoors and out. I'm also amazed at all the great-looking exterior lights, wall sconces, framed art, candles, and mirrors that can be added to instantly dress up an outdoor room.

ENTICE THE SENSES. I think the real fun of an indoor/outdoor room is that you can enjoy the wonderful sensory pleasures of a garden in a comfortable setting. Fragrant plants, the gentle sound of a water fountain, wind chimes, bird feeders, and an outdoor fireplace all engage the senses and heighten the emotional, physical, and spiritual connections to the natural world. These are some of the most intriguing elements in my garden rooms. They help to stimulate all of the senses and tap into the alluring qualities of the garden.

DAYLIGHT OR DARKNESS? It seems as though everyone is on the run these days. I find that when I do have the time to relax or entertain in the garden, it is often after the sun sets. And even with exterior lighting, my outdoor rooms look much different at night. So I started looking for container and border plants that would come into their own during the evening hours. Dark colors were swallowed up in dim light, so I created a nighttime garden using a mix of silver-gray and variegated foliage as well as pastel and white flowering plants that will glow in the moonlight. I also intermingled some intriguing flowers that open and release their fragrance after dark. Now the area seems to shimmer in the low light, inviting my guests to linger and enjoy the ambience.

*LEFT I used my "three-shape rule" for this eye-catching arrangement. 'Red Sensation' cordyline serves as my tall and spiky element, while 'Accent Mystic Mix' impatiens, 'Victory Pink Bronze Leaf' begonias, 'Tricolor' graptophyllum, and Japanese painted fern fill in the center for the round and full shape. Cascading over the edge is an airplane plant (*Chlorophytum comosum*).* *BELOW RIGHT The tray on this end table makes it easy to bring a pitcher and glasses in and out of the house.* *BELOW LEFT My shady porch is a favorite place to catch a cool breeze in the summertime.*

Simple Support for hyacinth bean vine

It has been a couple of months since I started the 'Ruby Moon' hyacinth bean vines from seed last spring. The seedlings are about a foot tall and ready to be set outside. The vines will help me dress up a rather drab wooden wall in the back of my garden, so I'm going to give them a little help to scale the wall by creating a string trellis.

materials

(40) 10d galvanized nails with heads

Ruler

Hammer

(1) roll of garden twine

(20) small sticks, 1 foot long (bamboo will also work)

'Ruby Moon' hyacinth bean vine seedlings

1. Prepare the soil at the base of the fence by digging down about 18 inches and adding amendments such as compost and peat moss to improve the drainage and fertility.

2. Drive nails along the top of the fence at 1-foot intervals and then repeat that pattern along the bottom so the bottom nails are directly below the ones at the top.

3. Tie the garden twine to the nail at the bottom corner and then connect it to the nail above, simply wrapping the twine several times around the nail. Then string it diagonally to the next nail at the bottom of the fence, creating a zigzag pattern. Continue this pattern to the end of the fence.

4. Plant a hyacinth bean vine seedling below each nail in the bottom row. Water the plants.

5. Insert a slender bamboo stick or branch by each plant to train it to grow onto the twine strands. Check the plants regularly to guide them up the twine, and keep them well watered. Within a few weeks the vines will cover the fence to create a beautiful veil of color.

twilight planter

This container project is designed for an evening garden to create a private oasis for you and your guests in the glow of candlelight. A prefabricated trellis is mounted in the planted container and functions as the background for the hanging votives. During the day, the trellis serves as a privacy screen and at night it magically transforms into a sparkling focal point. All the plants selected for this container will glow in the night. 'Diamond Frost' euphorbia has tiny white flowers that float above the plant. At night, the blooms look like hovering fireflies. 'Frosted Curls' sedge is an ornamental grass with soft, silvery green, recurving leaf blades that adds a nice textural element. When an evening breeze blows, the grasses move in the gentle wind. 'Blue Wonder' plectranthus has lovely medium blue blossoms that add a nice glimmer to the arrangement. It is a steady bloomer that looks great throughout the growing season.

materials

(1) 4 x 4-foot prefabricated trellis
(1) quart can of exterior latex paint
(1) 24-inch-diameter container
(2) 16-quart bags of potting soil
(2) 6-inch pots of 'Frosty Curls' sedge (*Carex albula*)
(1) 1-gallon pot of 'Blue Wonder' plectranthus
(3) 4-inch pots of 'Diamond Frost' euphorbia
(8) tea lights or votive candles
(8) glass votives or jars with a lip
1 roll of fine-gauge wire
Wire cutters
Needle-nose pliers
(1) box of galvanized 4-penny nails with heads
Hammer

1. Consider painting the trellis a color to coordinate with your container or setting; I used Sherwin-Williams "Turkish Coffee," which is a nice neutral hue. Use an exterior latex paint and let the trellis dry before putting it in the pot. Once the paint is dry, drive a nail into the crossbar positioned in the center of every other trellis opening so the candle votives will hang as pictured.

2. Place the large container where it will be displayed in the garden. Once it is potted up, it will be heavy and cumbersome to move.

3. Fill the container halfway with potting soil and insert the trellis.

4. Add more soil to the pot until the trellis is firmly anchored, but don't forget to leave room for the plants.

5. Position the ornamental grass in the front to spill over the edge with the euphorbia and plectranthus behind. I avoided adding a tall spiky element to this design because I didn't want any vegetation close to the votives. Remove the plants from their nursery pots and loosen their root balls; set them in place and add more soil to fill in around them. Then water them in.

6. With the trellis in place and the container planted, make the hanging votive jars. I used small votive holders with a lip just below the top, but any glass jar that can hold the candle will do. Take a long piece of wire (about 24 inches is good) and bend it around the jar just under the lip so that when suspended, it will hold the jar securely in place. With the needle-nose pliers twist the wire together close to the jar to tighten the ring. Leave just enough give in the wire so that you can thread another strand through to attach the handle.

continues on following pages

7. Make a handle over the mouth of the jar by bending the remaining wire into a loop and attaching it to the wire around the lip. Secure the wire by twisting it closed.

8. Hang a votive on each of the nails in the trellis and drop in a votive candle. At dusk, light the candles and watch your beautiful screen sparkle.

OPPOSITE *Silvery foliage and light-colored aromatic blossoms add shimmer and fragrance to an evening garden long after the sun has set.* **LEFT COLUMN, TOP TO BOTTOM** *Dusty miller (*Senecio cineraria*), lamb's ears 'Helen von Stein' (*Stachys byzantina*), silver spike (*Helichrysum thianschanicum*) and* Artemisia *'Silver Queen' are reliable twilight garden plants.* **RIGHT COLUMN, TOP TO BOTTOM** *Sweet aromas from flowering tobacco (*Nicotiana sylvestris*), lavender (*Lavandula angustifolia*), Oriental lily 'Casa Blanca', and Moonflower (*Ipomoea alba*) entice the senses as their light-colored blossoms glow in the dusk.*

PLANTS FOR THE EVENING GARDEN

- **Angels' trumpets** (*Brugmansia* spp.) Large trumpets that hang down from a fast-growing tropical plant; highly fragrant; white, peach, or yellow blooms; Zones 9–11.
- **Artemisia 'Silver Queen'** (*Artemisia ludoviciana*) 'Silver Queen') Silver-gray foliage; fresh scent; perennial; Zones 4–9.
- **Dusty miller** (*Senecio cineraria*) Silver-gray, low-growing, upright foliage; annual; Zones 8–10.
- **Flowering tobacco** (*Nicotiana sylvestris*) Small, white, tubular blooms that open at dusk emitting a strong, jasminelike fragrance; this short-lived perennial is grown as an annual; Zones 10–11.
- **Four o'clocks** (*Mirabilis jalapa*) Fragrant medium-size flowers; true to its name, this plant's blooms open in late afternoon; annual; Zones 8–11.
- **Gardenia** (*Gardenia augusta*) The queen of the fragrant garden; white blooms; strong fragrance; shrub; Zones 8–10.
- **Lamb's ears** 'Helen von Stein' (*Stachys byzantina* 'Helen von Stein') Silver-gray, woolly, large leaves; perennial; Zones 4–8.
- **Lavender** (*Lavandula angustifolia*) Light gray foliage; fresh scent; perennial; Zones 5–8.
- **Moonflower** (*Ipomoea alba*) Large, white blooms on a vining plant with heart-shaped leaves; lightly perfumed; blooms only at night; annual; Zones 9–11.
- **Night-blooming jessamine** (*Cestrum nocturnum*) Tropical shrub; indistinct white flowers that open at night; very strong fragrance that can be overpowering if it's planted too close to open windows, porches, or patios; Zones 8–9.
- **Oriental lily** 'Casa Blanca' Big, beautiful, pure white blooms; sweet fragrance; perennial bulb; Zones 4–8.
- **Silver spike** (*Helichrysum thianschanicum*) Shrubby upright plant with silver-gray foliage forms a 10- to 12-inch mound. Zones 8–10.
- **Sweet potato vine 'Margarita'** (*Ipomoea batatas*) Chartreuse foliage; annual vine/ground cover; Zones 9–11.
- **Variegated ribbon grass** (*Phalaris arundinacea* f. *variegata*) White and green variegated foliage; perennial; Zones 4–9.

SIGNATURE PLANT

1. 'Blue Wave' *H. macrophylla*
2. 'Tardiva' *H. paniculata*
3. 'Nikko Blue' *H. m.* (acidic soil)
4. 'Tardiva' *H. p.*
5. 'Ayesha' *H. m.*
6. 'Blue Wave' *H. m.* and 'Taube' *H. m.*
7. 'Nikko Blue' *H. m.* (alkaline soil)
8. 'Blue Wave' *H. m.* with 'Krossa Regal' hosta leaves
9. 'Lilacina' *H. m.*

Hydrangeas

I can remember as a child being drawn to the cool shaded area on the north side of the house where my mother had a large bank of stately blue hydrangeas. The giant blooms were as big as my head and such a clear, deep blue that they seemed as though they should be kept in a jewel box rather than casually hanging about the garden. At the time I had no idea there were so many varieties of hydrangeas available, all entrancing in their beauty. Since then, I have tried to squeeze as many as I could into my garden, including a selection of *Hydrangea paniculata* 'Tardiva', *H. arborescens* 'Annabelle', *H. quercifolia* (oakleaf hydrangea), *H. paniculata* 'Grandiflora' (PeeGee hydrangea), and *H. macrophylla* 'Endless Summer'.

1.
2.
3.
4.
5.
6.
7.
8.
9.

HYDRANGEA BLUES

Want to change the color of your mophead or snowball-shaped hydrangeas (*Hydrangea macrophylla*)? Add ¼ ounce of aluminum sulfate and ¼ ounce of sulfate of iron per 1 gallon of water. Water the hydrangea with this mixture, no more than 2 gallons per plant. For pink flowers, spread lime around the base of the shrub in spring and fall. Be patient; it may take a few growing seasons to see the change.

By the month of June all but two of the hydrangeas I grow are in their glory. The old PeeGee and the late-blooming 'Tardiva' have yet to come into full flower, but the garden is full of other hydrangea blooms. It seems that each year I discover a variety or two that I have never seen before and I always struggle to find a home for them. I suppose that if I had enough time and the right place for them, I could be easily lured into creating a hydrangea collection.

Keeping Hydrangeas Beautiful

Hydrangeas are easy to grow if you follow a few simple guidelines. Most varieties are cold-hardy to Zone 5, which means they will tolerate minimum winter temperatures between −10 and −20 degrees F. Check the plant tags or cultural information when choosing a hydrangea for your garden.

Hydrangeas are traditionally known as shade-garden plants, but too much shade can result in reduced bloom production. Ideally they should be situated in areas of light shade to partial sun. If you live in a cool climate, you can even plant them in full sun.

They also prefer to be in consistently moist, well-drained, humus-rich soil. A generous application of mulch will help keep the roots cool and retain moisture. Little pruning is required. In fact, improper pruning can result in bushes not producing any blooms. Old-fashioned hydrangeas set their flowers on the previous year's growth, or what is referred to as old wood. So, in late summer and early fall, your shrub is preparing blooms for next year and that's not the time to prune it. In early spring, you can tidy up the plant by removing any dead wood and old flower heads. Any severe cutting back should be done immediately after the flowers fade in the summer; any later, and you risk eliminating next year's blooms. New varieties, such as those in the 'Endless Summer' series, have flowers that bloom on old and new wood, so pruning is less of a concern for those shrubs.

If you are troubled by lack of blooms, the weather may also be the culprit. Harsh winter temperatures, warm spells followed by cold weather, and late freezes can damage or kill tender flower buds. If you site your plants in a north- or east-facing area of your garden, you can reduce the chances of the buds opening during aberrant warm winter weather. These areas of the garden warm up more slowly than southern or western exposures. Northern gardeners who know that they are in for a long cold spell can wrap their hydrangeas in burlap for winter protection. Planting the shrubs near house foundations also offers some refuge from cold temperatures.

I fertilize my hydrangeas twice during the summer with a slow-release fertilizer, normally in June and then again in August. In cooler climates this can be done once, usually in June. Follow the directions on the fertilizer package. Just remember that too much nitrogen will result in an abundance of lovely leaves at the expense of blooms.

OPPOSITE, LEFT *In early spring, I prune away dead wood and spent flowers on my mophead, lacecap, and oakleaf hydrangeas, but I'm careful not to cut away any stems with buds that formed last year. If those stems are pruned, my hydrangea will have few if any blooms to enjoy this summer.* RIGHT *'Blue Wave' lacecap hydrangea puts on quite a show.* BELOW *The cane above these emerging leaves is dead, so I can safely remove that portion of the stem.*

HYDRANGEA FAVORITES

- **'Ayesha'** Fragrant mophead variety with unique mauve petals shaped like little spoons.
- **'Forever Pink'** Compact 4-foot-tall plants with deep pink blooms; great for containers.
- **'Limelight'** Midsummer chartreuse flowers become pink and then turn to burgundy with cool fall temperatures.
- **'Nikko Blue'** Fabulous, deep blue large flowers; a true star in my garden.
- **'Sister Theresa'** White blooms tinged with pink.
- **'Sun Goddess'** Chartreuse foliage with traditional pink or blue blooms.

Saving the best to last

It's interesting how certain flowers evoke a sense of nostalgia: roses, hollyhocks, and dahlias, to name a few. But I find that whenever I talk about my hydrangeas to other gardeners, there are always many stories to share about our memories and experiences growing them. There's no question that these blooms are beautiful in the garden, and part of their appeal is that you can also preserve them for indoor arrangements.

You can dry fresh blooms in silica gel to retain their natural blue or pink color. Silica gel, available at most craft stores, is a sandy substance that absorbs moisture. A cost-saving method many floral arrangers are now using is to dry the flowers with cat litter instead of silica gel. They recommend using the finest-textured nonclumping cat litter available. I have not tried that method, so you may want to test it out on one bloom to see if you like the results.

It's best to dry one bloom per container, so you'll need to purchase several containers and more silica gel if you want to dry more than one bloom at a time.

materials

Large plastic bowls with lids
Silica gel (enough to fill the bowl) or cat litter
Scissors
Newspaper
Plastic bags

1. Use a plastic Tupperware-type container that is large enough to hold a flower without crushing it and a cup for sifting the silica gel over the bloom. The morning you are ready to begin drying the flowers, cut fresh, recently opened hydrangeas from the shrub. The petals should be dry. Cut stems very short so they will fit in the containers. A few leaves may be left on or all can be removed.

2. Place the hydrangea bloom in the container, upside down, on a thin layer of silica gel (stem facing up). Hold the flower above the layer of medium and gradually sift silica gel around the head. When about an inch of silica gel is holding the flower in place, you can release the bloom.

3. Work the silica gel into the center of the bloom and under all petals. When the first bloom is covered, if there is more room in the container, continue to layer whole or parts of flower heads with silica gel to within ½ inch of the container lid. Do not force them to fit in the container or they will be unnaturally shaped.

4. While sifting silica gel over the bloom, pay special attention to filling the edges of the container so that the medium will sift under the petals. Also, when the bloom is about half covered, gently knock the container to settle the silica gel around the petals.

5. Secure a lid on the container and label it with the date. Four days later pour the contents very slowly onto a newspaper and pluck out the dry hydrangeas. You can save the silica gel to reuse. Don't leave the hydrangeas in the silica gel for more than four days or they may become very brittle.

6. Gently tap the bloom clean and place it loosely in a plastic bag for storage until you're ready to use it. You may also lengthen the stem by taping a longer dry stem to it and placing the blossom in a vase. Storing the dried bloom in a vase keeps it from getting crushed in the bag.

grow a flower child

Once school is out for the summer, I enjoy inviting several of my friends and their children over for an afternoon of decorating and planting containers. It's a fun activity for everyone and a great way for kids to learn the basics of planting and caring for their own buckets of blooms.

When everyone arrives, the children dive into the fun by personalizing their own containers with stencils and markers. To keep things simple, I divide the plants into three groups—flowers, foliage, and fragrance—and let them choose a plant from each collection. After they fill their buckets with soil, they plant their container and label it as their own with a colorful plant name tag. Everyone gets a chance to see what others have made as they enjoy some special treats. The party food is presented in flowerpots that look as if they are filled with dirt and worms. At first the parents are a little dubious, but the kids really love the confections made from crushed chocolate cookies, pudding, and gummy worms. As the celebration winds down, the children take home their containers and a plastic watering can as a keepsake of the party.

materials

Amounts vary according to the number of children attending.

Metal buckets* (medium size—12-quart)

Exterior latex paint in bright colors*

Paintbrushes*

Drill and metal drill bit*

Worktables

Kraft paper or vinyl coverings for the tables

Stencils with various shapes: butterflies, flowers, etc.

Sharpie markers in bright primary colors

Masking tape

Large plastic plant markers

Child-size plastic watering cans

Potting soil

Large plastic storage containers for soil

Scoops for soil

Plants (4- to 6-inch pots work well—enough so each child can choose 3)

*Colorful plastic pails will also work. Create drainage holes in the bottom of the plastic containers using a nail and hammer.

before the day of the party

- Have all supplies on hand.
- Paint the buckets with an exterior latex paint formulated for metal. (I used Sherwin-Williams Dynamic Blue, Knockout Orange, Stop Red, and a yellow and a purple paint I had on hand.)
- Make drainage holes in the bottom of the buckets with a drill and metal bit.

continues on following pages

before guests arrive

- Set up two sets of tables—card tables with art supplies where children can personalize their buckets and long tables where kids can plant their containers.
- Protect the tables with kraft paper or vinyl tablecloths.
- Fill large plastic storage bins with potting soil.
- Arrange the nursery pots of plants into three groups (flowers, foliage, and fragrance) so children can pick one plant from each group for their container. (To simplify things, choose all sun-loving plants with bright flowers and colorful foliage.)
- Prepare and set out snacks.

when guests arrive

- Have the children select their buckets.
- Direct them to the table where stencils and markers are available so they can add their own decorations.
- Tape the stencils to the buckets before coloring them in.
- Have each child write his or her name on a large white plastic plant marker (to be placed in the buckets once it's planted).

Once the children have decorated their containers, have them set the buckets aside to let the stencils dry and invite them to have a snack. After the snack, divide the children into two groups. Invite one group to fill their buckets with soil from the plastic bin while the other group selects the plants they want to use. Then reverse the process.

The children can then take their buckets and plants to the planting tables, and with their parents' help, they plant their containers. This is an opportunity to talk to them about colors, textures, and the different needs of plants for sun, shade, and water. When they are finished, the children can water their planters using their own watering cans and add the labels with their name. It's fun to put all the finished containers on a table so everyone can see each other's designs.

special party treats

These terra-cotta pots of chocolate "dirt" and worms are always a hit with children.

- 2 large boxes chocolate instant pudding
- 2 cups milk
- 2 cups nondairy whipped topping
- 1 large package of dark chocolate sandwich cookies
- 1 package gummy worms
- Clear plastic cups (8-ounce size)
- 4-inch terra-cotta pots, new and washed
- Plastic spoons

Prepare the pudding mix and milk according to directions, and then fold the whipped topping into the pudding. Crush the cookies in a blender and mix half into the pudding mixture. Spoon the mixture into clear plastic cups that will fit into small terra-cotta pots. Then top with the remaining crushed cookie crumb "dirt." Place gummy worms on top of the cups. Slip the cups into the terra-cotta pots. (Makes 14 servings).

Other simple finger food: Dip—peanut butter and honey. Dippers—apples and bananas splashed with pineapple or lemon juice to keep them from discoloring. Platters of oatmeal cookies, sticks of string cheese, bite-size Ritz crackers and Goldfish crackers, and gelatin jigglers. Pitchers of lemonade and fruit punch.

When choosing plants for your party, look for those with fun flower shapes, colorful leaves, great textures, and wonderful fragrance. Here are some of the plants I've used.

- **Colorful flowers:** Periwinkle (*Vinca* spp.), bat-faced cuphea (*Cuphea llavea*), cigar plant (*Cuphea ignea*), Mexican false heather (*Cuphea hyssopifolia*), angelonia (*Angelonia angustifolia*), 'Dragonwing' begonias, 'Profusion' zinnias, shrimp plant (*Justicia* spp.), impatiens, pentas (*Pentas lanceolata*), petunias (*Petunia* x *hybrida*), marigolds (*Tagetes* spp.).
- **Foliage:** 'Black Dragon' coleus (*Coleus* x *hybridus* 'Black Dragon'), creeping Jenny (*Lysimachia* spp.), sweet potato vine (*Ipomoea batatas*), purple heart (*Tradescantia pallida*), airplane plant (*Chlorophytum comosum*), lamb's ears (*Stachys* spp.), foxtail asparagus fern (*Asparagus densiflorus* 'Myersii'), Mexican feather grass (*Nassella tenuissima*). (I make sure there is enough lamb's ears and feather grass for everyone, since kids usually go for those and we don't want anyone left out.)
- **Fragrance:** Variegated Cuban oregano (*Plectranthus amboinicus* 'Variegatus'), chocolate mint (*Mentha* x *piperita* cvs.), cinnamon basil (*Ocimum basilicum* 'Cinnamon'), lemon basil (*O. basilicum* 'Citriodorum'), rosemary (*Rosmarinus officinalis*), sage (*Salvia* spp.), bronze fennel (*Foeniculum vulgare* 'Bronze'), Korean mint (*Agastache rugosa*), pennyroyal (*Mentha* spp.), scented geraniums (*Pelargonium* spp.)

SIGNATURE PLANT

1. 'Golden Stargazer'
2. 'La Reine', 'Sacramento', and 'Pollyanna'
3. 'Lollipop'
4. 'Montreaux'
5. 'Chianti'
6. 'Le Reine'
7. 'Sacramento'
8. 'Black Beauty'
9. 'Navona'

Garden Lilies

Lilies rightfully hold the title as the Grande Dames of the summer cottage garden. They are showy, vibrant, and often exquisitely perfumed. Hundreds of varieties have been hybridized and grouped into three major categories: Asiatic, Trumpet, and Oriental. Each group has its own special qualities and period of flowering, which overlaps throughout the growing season. By planting selections from each group, you can enjoy an uninterrupted show of color from early summer to frost.

1.
2.
3.
4.
5.
6.
7.
8.
9.

ASIATIC LILIES are first to break bud in early summer, opening in an array of bright and pastel shades that are often "freckled" with dark spots. They come in both short and tall varieties (2 to 5 feet), making them easy to mix with other plants in flower borders. The 'Pixie' series are dwarf types (1 to 2 feet) that are perfect for containers. Although Asiatic are not as fragrant as Trumpet or Oriental lilies, they are the easiest to grow, and they are known to be wonderfully reliable and will multiply quickly.

TRUMPET LILIES, also known as Aurelian hybrids, are lanky by comparison (4 to 8 feet) and bloom in midsummer with spotless, fused petals. Placed in the middle and back of the border, each stem displays up to a dozen dazzling flowers. Thanks to new hybrids, the once limited color palette of Trumpet lilies has greatly expanded.

ORIENTAL LILIES, flamboyant and sweetly scented (3 to 6 feet tall), adorn the garden from midsummer to fall and can be counted on to end the season with a bang. Plate-sized exotic flowers, up to 9 inches across, offer splashy shades of white, pink, and crimson with reflexed, or backward-curving, petals that may be spotted, brushed, or edged with contrasting colors. Oriental lilies put on their best show when protected from the hot afternoon sun and strong winds.

LILY REQUIREMENTS

- **Light:** Full sun, filtered light, or afternoon shade. Lilies like "cool feet," so mix them with low-growing plants to keep the roots shaded.
- **Wind protection:** Avoid windy sites. Staking helps.
- **Soil:** Deep, loose, well-drained fertile soil.
- **Mulch:** 2 to 3 inches of organic mulch.
- **Water:** Consistently moist to about 6 inches deep, but not soggy.
- **Fertilizer:** In spring, when plants reach 6 inches tall, apply a complete slow-release bulb fertilizer.

Planting Lily Bulbs

In spring or fall, plant only firm bulbs with fresh, white roots. Keep bulbs in damp peat moss or the crisper drawer in the refrigerator until ready to plant.
1) Dig a generous hole 12 inches deeper than the planting depth and work in ample organic matter.
2) Plant at a depth three times the height of the bulb.
3) Set the bulbs with the roots fanned out.
4) Space the bulbs 6 to 12 inches apart for massed effect.

Cut Lilies

Lilies make long-lasting cut flowers; however, take no more than one-third of the stem so the plant's foliage can build up energy in the bulb for next year's blooms. Once the stalk yellows, cut it to the ground or leave it to mark the bulb's location.

Lily pollen can stain clothing, upholstery, and tablecloths. When handling cut lilies, remove the pollen-laden stamens by giving them a gentle tug.

If pollen settles on fabric, don't wet the stain. Press the sticky side of a piece of tape against the pollen and gently pull the tape back to lift pollen from the fabric. Then set the fabric in the sun for an hour or so.

Colorful Combinations

Lilies are quite companionable with other perennials, as well as with annuals and shrubs. Here are some color-themed planting suggestions.

COOL COLOR MIX

'Pandora' lily

'Crimson Pigmy' purple barberry shrub (*Berberis thunbergii* f. *atropurpurea*)

Purple iris

'Classic Passion Patriot' lantana

MOSTLY WHITE DISPLAY

'Casa Blanca' lily

Lamb's ears (*Stachys byzantina*)

'Angelface White' angelonia

'Supertunia Blushing Princess' petunia

HOT COLOR MIX

'Sacramento' lily

Red geranium

'Sky Fire' coleus

'Tiddley Winks Yellow' lantana

'Little Red Riding Hood' purple fountain grass (*Pennisetum alopecuroides* 'Little Red Riding Hood')

'Royal Velvet' petunias

OTHER LILY COMPANIONS

'Festival Star' gypsophila—clouds of dainty white flowers

'Broadway Lights' leucanthemum—3-inch flowers that turn from yellow to white

'Jolly Bee' geranium—lasting blue blooms

'Laguna Trailing Lilac' lobelia—low grower around the base of lilies

'Soprano Purple' osteospermum—daisylike flowers

'Stratosphere Pink Picotee' gaura—airy look to frame the lilies

ABOVE RIGHT *The nodding blossoms of white and lemon 'Time Out' lilies and orange 'Norwich Canary' crocosmia are a natural mix.* **RIGHT** *Soft pink 'Vivaldi' Asiatic lilies blend beautifully with 'Miss Kim's Knee High' coneflower. Purple perilla, pink zinnias, Polish amaranth, and 'Indigo Spires' salvia also serve as companions to the lilies.*

pick your pleasure

To make sure I have enough lilies indoors and out, I like to pack several varieties of Asiatic lily bulbs into a 4 x 4-foot framed bed. This gives me a concentration of blooms for a big show of color in the garden and supplies me with plenty of cut flowers for arrangements.

The first time I tried this, the lilies grew to their 36-inch height and the flowers opened, only to be blown over in a summer storm. So the next year I gave them some extra support by crisscrossing the bed with a short fence made from pruned branches. Bamboo or any type of flexible pole would likewise suffice. It was an easy solution that worked like a charm. This support system could also be used for other tall plants that grow in a grouping like this.

materials

(12) 4-foot-long branches, 2 inches in diameter
(20) 6-foot-long branches, 1 inch in diameter
Hammer
Long-handled pruner
Pruning saw

1. Cut the branches to the lengths needed.

2. Hammer the 4-foot-long stakes about 2 feet apart in a diagonal line from corner to corner. Make sure they are driven deep enough so they are anchored firmly in the ground.

3. Lay the first 6-foot-long branch of the fence diagonally across the bed, weaving it in and out of the stakes. Lay the next branch along the other line, again weaving it in and out between the stakes.

4. For the second layer, do the same as step 3, but weave the branches on the opposite side of the stakes from the first layer.

5. Continue this pattern until the fence is roughly 18 inches high.

6. Use the long-handled pruner to trim the ends of the branches at each corner. For my all-lily display, I mixed Asiatic varieties of 'Brunello' (orange), 'Nove Centro' (yellow), 'Pollyana' (yellow with flecks), and 'Soirée' (dark orange with flecks) lilies and planted the bulbs 6 inches apart.

growing garden art

By midsummer, while much of my time is spent keeping my garden watered, mulched, and pruned, I find myself looking for ways to heighten its visual interest. One project that makes a great garden embellishment is an ivy topiary. You'll find that by starting with large plants such as the 6-inch pots of ivy, your topiary will fill in within one growing season.

materials

(1) 18-inch iron urn (or any other container of your choice)

(1) 24-inch-tall cone-shaped topiary form (available at antiques shops, craft stores, online, etc.)

(2) 16-quart bags of potting soil

(3) 6-inch pots of variegated ivy (your choice)

Green dental floss

Shears or gardening scissors

Watering can

Liquid fertilizer

1. Fill the container with potting soil, leaving about 3 inches of space below the rim of the container.

2. Secure the topiary form in the center of the container by burying several inches of the base beneath the potting soil. Besides the cone-shaped form I used for this particular project, there are other shapes and sizes available. Just be sure to select a container that is proportional to the form you select.

3. Plant the ivies around the base of the form. Position the plants so that the longest tendrils are closest to it.

4. Wind the plant tendrils up the form and loosely secure with green dental floss.

5. After planting, water the vines in and feed them with an all-purpose liquid fertilizer diluted according to the package directions.

6. As the vines grow, I continue to train them and, as they fill out the form, clip them to maintain the shape.

CLOCKWISE FROM TOP RIGHT *A long flowering period and 6-inch-wide blooms make 'Barbara Mitchell' a favorite daylily among gardeners. Common daylilies known as tawny lily or "ditch lily" naturalize easily and are often found blooming along roadsides; the orange blossoms make a natural pairing with purple coneflowers, a native wildflower indigenous to the Great Plains. The peachy pink blossoms of 'Hall's Pink' lily bloom through a veil of 'Indigo Spires' salvia. Towering up to 6 feet tall, 'Autumn Minaret' daylilies begin to flower about midsummer and usually don't quit until fall.*

Daylilies

Creating a living piece of garden art is a great diversion from some of the more mundane summer gardening tasks such as weeding and mowing. As I get back to the tasks at hand, I find myself searching the borders to see what's about to bloom next in the garden. I don't have to wait long. My daylilies are starting to open.

These spectacular bloomers should come with a warning: Daylilies can be habit-forming! Once you have grown them in your garden, you'll know firsthand why they have such an enthusiastic following. I count myself among the millions of gardeners who are daylily devotees. And why not: There are more than 52,000 cultivars available in a rainbow of colors, shapes, and sizes, and the plants nearly take care of themselves. Since they are drought resistant and adaptable to nearly any soil and light conditions, I can plant them anywhere I need a splash of color. And by combining early-, mid-, and late-season bloomers, I can make the colorful flower display last from late spring through autumn. These adaptable perennials come back year after year and grow in size, so you can divide and share them with others. Talk about your ideal plant!

The botanical name for daylily is *Hemerocallis,* which is Greek for "beautiful for a day" and hints at the plant's special charm. Each bloom lives and dies in the course of a day, but since a single plant produces lots of buds, its flowering display goes on for weeks.

Daylilies were originally found in temperate parts of Asia, but over the span of centuries they have been exported and transplanted into gardens throughout the world. In the 1930s the pioneering work of plant breeders in the United States and England created several "breakthrough" cultivars that added amazing variations to the plant's original form. Today daylilies can be found in sizes that range from minis to varieties that grow nearly 5 feet tall. Flower shapes are available in circular, triangular, ruffled, double, spider, star, flat, recurved, or trumpet forms. And while earlier colors were limited to yellow, orange, and red, you now have a crayon boxful of colors to choose from. Though I find the new hybrids beautiful, I must confess that I have a weakness for the graceful qualities and sweet aroma of the old-fashioned varieties. Many of them have long stems, or scapes, that elevate the flowers high above the foliage. The blooms are loose and relaxed looking, giving them a certain elegance that modern varieties seem to lack.

Whether you prefer the newer, hybrid varieties or the old-fashioned favorites, daylilies are excellent for slopes, massed in beds, and along foundations. I've found that the white, yellow, and pastel cultivars show their best color in full sun, while darker varieties favor light shade during the hottest part of the day.

In my garden I've had good results combining compact varieties with 'Superbells' calibrachoas, 'Catalina' torenia, and 'Supertunia' petunias. They also look great in front of climbing roses. The taller varieties complement 'Magnus' purple coneflowers (*Echinacea*), 'Summer Pastels' yarrow (*Achillea*), tall summer phlox, and drumstick alliums.

PLANTING AND CARE TIPS

In the northern part of the country, the ideal planting time is spring to early summer. In the South, plant in early spring or late fall.

Although daylilies aren't particular about soil conditions, I like to add compost into my clay soil to loosen it up and improve drainage. Mound up the planting area about an inch higher than the surrounding area so rainwater will run off. The crown of the plant (where the leaves and roots meet) should be no more than ½ inch below the surface.

Water regularly during the first growing season to establish an extensive root system. For a neat appearance, remove old stalks and divide the clumps every 2 to 3 years in early spring.

1. Persian shield
2. 'Red-Stem' colocasia
3. Tropical hibiscus and red bouvardia
4. 'Frydek' alocasia
5. Lily of the Nile
6. 'Alice Du Pont' mandevilla
7. 'Charles Grimaldi' brugmansia
8. 'Albomarginata' xanthosoma
9. Copper plant

Tropical Plants

Nothing says summer like tropical plants. They conjure up images of exotic, hot, and faraway places. You can give an area of your garden a "vacation feel" by adding lots of tropical beauties, many of which are a natural combination with water features. If you are hesitant to try some of these big, bold plants because you live in a region where it freezes in winter, take heart. Just choose plants that are easy to maintain as houseplants or those that you can dig up and store over the winter.

1.
2.
3.
4.
5.
6.
7.
8.
9.

Summer's End and Spring's Beginning

If I had to choose one word to define summer's end, it would be *abundance*. It is the season when gardens are full of food and flowers. At last, there are too many tomatoes to eat in one sitting and enough to share among friends. A myriad of community celebrations and summer fairs proudly exhibit the bounty of the season.

With cooler temperatures and more abundant rains promised in the days ahead, I feel the burden of watering, mowing, and maintaining the garden let up. Though I'm sorry to see the season end, I breathe a sigh of relief that the pace will be changing in the fall.

The marvelous thing about the seasons is their revolving nature. No sooner than one season ends, we are reminded of more to come. Beginning in the middle of summer the catalogs of spring-flowering bulbs start arriving, reminding me to start thinking about spring. But before I sit down to make my order, I first want to gather up seeds that are ready to be harvested from ripened flower heads.

Not too many years ago, if you wanted to have a garden from one year to the next you had to save seeds. Vegetable and flower seeds were vital to farm life, and exchanging them with neighbors and friends was an important part of rural culture. Today, with so many seeds available to us from garden centers and mail-order catalogs, it may seem a bit pointless to try to gather them. But I still collect some from my garden. I find it is one of the best ways to preserve an unusual or hard-to-find plant variety. My basket flowers were spectacular just a few weeks ago. Since the seeds are difficult to find, I save as many as I can. And if you have a thrifty side like I do, you know that the cost of buying seeds can really add up, so why not save a little money? It seems that seed companies are including fewer and fewer seeds in a packet, and if you have a large area to cover, harvesting your own supply certainly helps the bottom line.

If you want to collect and replant the seeds of a particular plant, just tag the most vigorous and colorful flowers with a piece of bright yarn and allow them to set seed heads. The pods are ready for harvesting when they are dry and brittle, but before they break open. On a dry, sunny day, after the dew has evaporated, remove the seed heads with pruners and place them on a sheet of newspaper laid out in a tray. Be sure not to combine different types of seed heads in the same tray unless you plan on planting them together. If the seed heads are breaking open as you cut them, lay a newspaper on the ground to collect the falling seeds. Add those to the heads on the paper-lined tray. Place the tray in a warm, dry spot. As the heads continue to dry, the seeds will fall out of the pods. You may need to gently shake or coax all the seeds out with your fingers. It is important that the seeds are thoroughly dry before you store them. At that point it is just a matter of collecting and storing them in labeled, airtight plastic bags or jars.

I save seeds from a wide range of my old garden standbys, plants such as my Formosa lily (*Lilium formosum*), verbena-on-a-stick (*Verbena bonariensis*), and even flowering tobacco (*Nicotiana*). I avoid collecting seeds from hybrid varieties because these plants don't always come back true from seeds.

After I gather and store my seeds for next season, I close out the summer by getting my order for spring-flowering bulbs in the mail. There's something both hopeful and a little melancholy about ordering spring bulbs. I am excited about the possibilities of growing new varieties of daffodils, tulips, and hyacinths, but there is that twinge of sadness about saying good-bye to all that summer has provided.

autumn.

Here's a riddle I've puzzled over for years: What day marks the beginning of autumn? If I had to point to a single date on the calendar, it would be June 21, the day of the summer solstice. Now, you may think that the first "official" day of summer can't be the beginning of fall. On the day of the summer solstice the sun's path reaches its highest arc, showering us with more minutes of daylight than we've had all year. But for each day that follows (until December 21) the sun sinks lower in the sky, the light dims, and the minutes between sunrise and sunset become fewer. So for me, the summer solstice marks the first shift toward autumn.

My goal from the summer solstice on is to take full advantage of each ray of sunshine and turn it into a flower. To do that, I peer at my summer garden through a botanical crystal ball and try to capture a glimpse of the future. First I look at what I have growing in the garden. Each summer is different due to the weather conditions and the plants I'm growing that year, so some parts of the garden thrive better than others. I evaluate what looks good and judge which plants will keep performing into the fall. Those are the plants I'll keep. By midsummer there are perennials that are bowing out, leggy-looking annuals, and bug-bitten foliage. I'll cut back anything that holds the promise of reviving, but if a plant looks weak and hopeless, out it goes. And since I don't want my garden to miss a beat, I start thinking about what I need to add to keep the visual interest high. It's often an equation that works out something like this: my summer border in late June, minus any plants that are past their prime, plus at least five more fall beauties, equals one glorious fall garden.

To help you pick out plants for your fall garden, I've put together a list of some of my favorite perennials, annuals, ornamental grasses, and even some fall-blooming bulbs that I rely on to help charge things up.

These are the plants I've come to rely on to build a full crescendo of color right up to the first hard freeze. Autumn is not a time to be shy about color. I like to match the majesty of the fall landscape by filling my borders to the brim with jewel-toned hues.

My favorite seasonal celebration is a gathering of friends who come by the garden to sample some unique apples. Autumn is the time when apple trees are laden with sweet, fresh fruit, and I've found a great mail-order source that ships just-picked heritage varieties that you won't find in the supermarket. The sampler box is delivered with a page describing the history and lore of each apple, so the afternoon is spent tasting the fruits and learning about each variety's colorful past.

As dipping temperatures foretell the final shift to winter, I pull out all the stops and buy a trunkload of pumpkins, gourds, and mums and have fun decorating my porch, loggia, steps, and walkways with these classic symbols of the season.

Autumn's Roll Call

Around the first of August, I usually hear what I've come to think of as the first sound of autumn. It is the rapid, loud, pulsing "ree-ree-ree" song that the male cicadas plaintively sing to their silent mates. I think of this sound as nature's early warning system proclaiming that while summer is still here, fall is on its way. I must admit that when I first hear the cicadas call, my heart skips a beat. It's my signal that it's time to get going on all the things I want to accomplish before the first frost. To help keep me on track, I make a list of things to do. List making is one of my favorite pasttimes. I fill any idle moment jotting down garden reminders, but my favorite time to embrace this task is in the early morning, sitting on my loggia with my first cup of coffee; or if I'm traveling, while I'm at the airport waiting for a flight, thinking about what I want to do next time I'm home in the garden. Although a few things on my fall to-do list change from year to year, there are some basic tasks that always appear. These might be useful to you as well.

ABOVE *As I empty containers of their summer blooms, I replant them with plenty of spring flowering bulbs.* **LEFT** *Cooler temperatures and fewer hours of daylight mean it's time to freshen up the borders with mums and other colorful fall plants.*

TO DO LIST

PLANTING

- ☐ Seed new lawn areas or patch thin areas. Keep newly seeded areas moist until grass is established.
- ☐ Take cuttings of geraniums, begonias, impatiens, coleus, and other tender plants for overwintering on the windowsill.
- ☐ As plants go dormant, but before the ground freezes, transplant trees and shrubs that you want to relocate. After they shed their leaves, moving trees and shrubs is less of a shock on the plants and the roots will still grow until colder temperatures set in. Keep the roots from drying out by wrapping them in a plastic sheet and keep the plants well watered until you can move them to their new home.
- ☐ If you live in a region with relatively mild winters (Zones 7 and warmer), plant pansies, violas, and kale. They will bloom from now until hot temperatures set in next spring. Refresh tired-looking plants in containers and borders with fall bloomers. For a list of plants to consider, see page 114.
- ☐ Plant spring-flowering bulbs such as tulips, daffodils, and crocuses. Arrange them in groups of 15 to 20 of the same variety for the most dramatic result.
- ☐ Plant peonies. In warmer climates, I've had luck with the varieties 'Festiva Maxima' and 'Sarah Bernhardt'. Also, look for new varieties developed to have stronger stems.
- ☐ Choose and plant new trees and shrubs. Keep them well watered throughout the fall and make sure they're mulched.
- ☐ If you live where the ground freezes in winter, lift gladioli, dahlias, cannas, and tuberous begonias after frost, brush the soil off, and store them in peat moss or sawdust in a cool area for winter.
- ☐ Pot up herbs in small containers for the kitchen windowsill, pinching back the stems to compensate for root loss and to encourage compact growth. Try parsley, thyme, mint, chives, oregano, or basil.

CLEAN UP

- ☐ If Japanese beetles have been a problem in the garden, chances are the grubs (they look like short, fat white worms) are living in the soil. A long-lasting solution is to treat the area with milky spores. Check the Source Guide, page 209, for sources.
- ☐ Cut back perennial foliage after a killing freeze. Select plants to cut back that have had disease problems during the growing season, but allow stems and seed heads that will provide food for birds or winter interest to remain intact.
- ☐ Rake leaves and add them to the compost bin. (Instructions on how to build a compost corral can be found on page 156.)
- ☐ Build up the soil in the flower beds by working in plenty of compost.

TOOLS AND MAINTENANCE

- ☐ Keep up with the weeding. Unwanted plants are energetically attempting to set seed.
- ☐ Before you put away your mower, weed whip, leaf blower, or other gasoline-powered equipment, run the engine until it is dry or drain the gasoline. Take the equipment to the shop for any repairs needed.
- ☐ Clean and oil garden tools. I store my tools in a 5-gallon bucket filled with sand and about a cup of mineral oil to keep them clean and oiled.
- ☐ Drain outside water lines, turn off faucets, and bring in hoses.
- ☐ Clean and store terra-cotta containers, which may crack in freezing temperatures. Small pots can be sterilized by soaking them in a solution of 1 part bleach to 4 parts water.
- ☐ Hang and fill bird feeders. Place them in areas where you can enjoy watching the birds visit, but that also provide protection and safe places to perch.

march
april
may
june
july
august
september
october
november
december
january
february

EARLY AUTUMN

FAVORITE FALL PLANTS

PERENNIALS

'Angelina' sedum (*Sedum rupestre* 'Angelina')
Arkansas amsonia (*Amsonia hubrectii*)
Autumn fern (*Dryopteris erythrosora*)
'Autumn Fire' sedum (*Sedum hylotelephium* 'Autumn Fire')
Autumn sage (*Salvia greggii*)
'Bluebird' smooth aster (*Aster laevis*)
'Catlin's Giant' ajuga (*Ajuga reptans* 'Catlin's Giant')
'Chocolate' snakeroot (*Eupatorium rugosum* 'Chocolate')
Chrysanthemum (*Chrysanthemum* x *morifolium*)
'Fireworks' goldenrod (*Solidago rugosa* 'Fireworks')
Hardy ageratum (*Eupatorium*)
Hardy begonia (*Begonia grandis*)
Helenium (*Helenium autumnale*)
Hosta (*Hosta* spp.)
'Indigo Spires' salvia (*Salvia* 'Indigo Spires')
Japanese anemone (*Anemone* x *hybrida*)
Mexican sage (*Salvia leucantha*)
Monkshood (*Aconitum*)
'October Skies' aster (*Aster oblongifolius*)
Perennial sunflower (*Helianthus* x *multiflorus*)
'Petit Blue' caryopteris (*Caryopteris* x *clandonensis* 'Petit Blue')
Plume poppies (*Macleaya* spp.)
'Powis Castle' artemisia (*Artemisia* 'Powis Castle')
'Purple Dome' New England aster (*Aster novae-angliae* 'Purple Dome')
Royal fern (*Osmunda regalis*)
Solomon's seal (*Polygonatum*)
'Sunshine Blue' caryopteris (*C.* x *clandonensis* 'Sunshine Blue')
Sweet autumn clematis (*Clematis texensis*)
Toad lily (*Tricyrtis* spp.)

ANNUALS

'Blackie' or 'Margarita' sweet potato vine (*Ipomoea batatas* 'Blackie' or *I. batatas* 'Margarita')
Calibrachoa (*Calibrachoa* spp.)
Cockscomb (*Celosia argentea*)
Coleus (*Coleus* x *hybridus*)
Hyacinth bean vine (*Dolichos lablab*)
Lantana (*Lantana* spp.)
Marigold (*Tagetes* spp.)
Morning glory (*Ipomoea* spp.)
Ornamental cabbage and kale (*Brassica oleracea*)
Ornamental peppers (*Capsicum annum*)
Petunias (*Petunia* x *hybrida*)
Violas and pansies (*Viola* spp.)
Torenia (*Torenia fournieri*)

ORNAMENTAL GRASSES

'Cabaret' miscanthus (*Miscanthus* 'Cabaret') or 'Morning Light' miscanthus (*M. sinensis* 'Morning Light')
'Evergold' carex (*Carex hachijoensis* 'Evergold')
'Karl Foerster' feather reed grass (*Calamagrostis* x *acutiflora* 'Karl Foerster')
'Hameln' dwarf fountain grass (*Pennisetum* 'Hameln')
'Heavy Metal' switch grass (*Panicum virgatum* 'Heavy Metal')
Leatherleaf sedge (*Carex buchananii*)
Mexican feather grass (*Stipa tenuissima*)
Muhly grass (*Muhlenbergia*)
Ribbon grass (*Phalaris arundinacea*)
'Toffee Twist' carex (*Carex flagellifera* 'Toffee Twist')

BULBS

Autumn crocus (*Crocus speciosus*)
Colchicum (*Colchicum autumnale*)
Lycoris (*Lycoris radiata*)
Nerine (*Nerine* spp.)
Sternbergia (*Sternbergia lutea*)

DISCOVER COLCHICUMS

An autumn beauty that few gardeners seem to know about is a large fall-blooming bulb called colchicum (*Colchicum autumnale*). Planted in August, colchicums bloom in as little as 4 weeks. I love the translucent quality of their petals, and I plant them in clumps to create a veil of color hinting at the seasonal transition that's about to happen. The bulb is often confused with autumn crocus, but in fact the colchicum is not a crocus but a perennial herb in the lily family (Liliaceae). Colchicum's flowers arise from bulblike corms that should be planted as soon as they arrive in late summer or early fall. (If not planted immediately, the corms frequently bloom during storage.) Plant them in well-drained soil in full sun to partial shade. Good planting sites include naturalized areas under the filtered shade of large trees and shrubs, in rock gardens, or in low-growing ground covers such as sedum. The corms should be planted 2 to 3 inches deep and 6 inches apart. I've grown hybrids such as 'Waterlily', 'Album', and 'Lilac Wonder'. Sources for colchicums are listed in the Source Guide (see page 209).

SIGNATURE PLANT

1. 'Paul' *S. van houttei*
2. 'Raspberry Ripple' *S. greggi*
3. 'Coral Nymph' *S. coccinea*
4. 'Santa Barbara' Mexican sage *S. leucantha*
5. Mexican sage and 'Indigo Spires' salvia
6. 'Indigo Spires' salvia
7. 'Lady in Red' *S. coccinea*
8. Mealycup sage, *S. farinacea*
9. Scarlet sage *S. splendens*

Salvia

I'm constantly looking for plants that will sing in my garden for a long time, particularly ones that can help me carry the tune between summer and fall. Salvias are plants that always seem to be in perfect pitch. They are long blooming and drought tolerant and come in a range of vibrant colors. Salvias, or sages as they are known to some, are the largest genus in the mint family (Lamiacea), with more than 100 varieties available throughout the country. Depending on the plants you select and your growing zone, they can be used in a variety of ways: as annual bedding plants, border perennials, culinary herbs, container plants, or ground covers. Once they are established, about all I do to encourage continued blooming is remove spent blossoms and tip-pinch shoots to maintain their form.

1.
2.
3.
4.
5.
6.
7.
8.
9.

Salvia and ornamental pepper containers

Small-size salvias are the perfect companions in containers. This design is my salute to summer's end and fall's beginning. It combines 'Victoria Blue' mealycup sage (*Salvia farinacea*), a collection of plants that showcases summer blooms and foliage, and an ornamental pepper to create a color palette that embraces autumn. 'Victoria' offers deep purple/blue flowers and has a wonderfully long blooming period, and its mature height of only 18 inches keeps it from overshadowing other plants.

plants

(2) quart-size pots of 'Victoria Blue' mealycup sage (*Salvia farinacea* 'Victoria Blue')

(2) quart-size pots of 'Red Missile' ornamental peppers (*Capsicum annuum* 'Red Missile')

(4) 3-inch nursery pots of compact zinnias such as 'Swizzle', 'Profusion Orange', or 'Zowie Yellow Flame'

(3) 3-inch nursery pots of variegated lilyturf (*Liriope muscari* 'Variegata')

(6) plugs of dark blue violas

(1) quart-size pot of burgundy coleus

I created this design knowing that the plants would not have a full growing season to mature, so I really packed them in for instant impact. Don't be afraid to use a lot of plants. After all, fall is your last chance to create a big splash of color in the garden before winter sets in.

materials

(1) wire basket 8 inches tall and 13 inches in diameter

(1) saucer to fit under the basket

(1) 16-quart bag of potting soil

(1) bag of sheet moss

(1) bucket of water

(1) plastic bag

1. Soak the sheet moss in a bucket of water for about 15 minutes. The water will refresh the moss and also makes it easier to work with.

2. Simply lay the pieces of moss inside the basket and gently push them into the openings to secure them in place. Overlap the pieces to create a thick layer.

3. Next, cut a piece of plastic bag to fit inside the basket. Poke a couple of holes through the plastic for drainage.

4. Fill the basket about halfway with potting soil.

5. Arrange the plants in the basket and add more soil around them, tamping the soil firmly as you go. The top of the soil line should be 1 to 2 inches from the lip, so that water will pool without spilling over the sides. Put a saucer under the container to catch the water as it drains through.

march
april
may
june
july
august
september
october
november
december
january
february

EARLY AUTUMN

Drying Summer Flowers

My first real sign that autumn has arrived usually catches me off guard. Often it happens just as I'm walking out of my back door thinking about the day's schedule when out of the blue, it hits me—a wave of cool fresh air that has that unmistakable feeling of fall. That's my cue that it's time to gather up armloads of flowers and grasses and preserve their beauty awhile longer by drying them. It's a simple and low-tech way of bringing the garden indoors during fall.

Not all plants are well suited for drying, but there are groups identified as "everlastings" that are known for their ability to hold their color and shape in a dried form. By experimenting over the years, I've found those and a few more that I like to dry and use in floral arrangements.

FLOWERS FOR DRYING

- Baby's breath (*Gypsophila* spp.)
- Bachelor's buttons (*Centaurea* spp.)
- Bells of Ireland (*Moluccella laevis* spp.)
- Blue sage (*Salvia* spp.)
- Cockscomb/celosia (*Celosia* spp.)
- Globe amaranth (*Gomphrena* spp.)
- Hydrangea (*Hydrangea* spp.)
- Larkspur (*Consolida ajacis*)
- Roses (*Rosa* spp.)
- Sea lavender (*Limonium* spp.)
- Statice (*Limonium* spp.)
- Strawflower (*Helichrysum* spp.)
- Yarrow (*Achillea* spp.; yellow varieties are best)

SEED HEADS FOR DRYING

- Bittersweet (*Celastrus* spp.)
- Blackberry lily (*Belamcanda* spp.)
- Cattail (*Typha domingensis*)
- Chinese lantern (*Physalis* spp.)
- Coneflower (*Echinacea* spp.)
- Honesty, money plant (*Lunaria annua*)
- Iris (*Iris* spp.)
- Love-in-a-mist (*Nigella* spp.)
- Milkweed (*Asclepias* spp.)
- Poppy (*Papaver* spp.)
- Queen Anne's lace (*Daucus carota* spp. *carota*)
- Starflower (*Scabiosa stellata*)

GRASSES FOR DRYING

- Eulalia grass (*Miscanthus sinensis* 'Gracillimus')
- Fountain grass (*Pennisetum alopecuroides*)
- 'Morning Light' miscanthus (*Miscanthus sinensis* 'Morning Light')
- Spike grass (*Achnatherum calamagrostis*)
- Zebra grass (*Miscanthus sinensis* 'Zebrinus')

Experience is the best teacher, so if there are plants in your garden that you want to dry, I say go for it. Gather blossoms when they are looking their best. I like to cut them late in the morning after the dew has dried and before they become wilted from the heat and sun. Bouquets are more interesting if the dried flowers are at different stages of development, from buds to fully open blossoms, so look for those stages as you select your flowers. I've found that blue, orange, and pink flowers hold their colors best. Sometimes I don't have time to strip the leaves and bundle the flowers immediately, so I just keep them in a bucket of lukewarm water in a cool, dry place, but I try to get to them that same day.

When I'm ready, I remove the leaves and use rubber bands to bundle together the same variety of flowers into small groups. Make sure the rubber bands are tight so that as the stems dry they will continue to constrict around them. It's best to dry large flowers such as hydrangeas individually.

Hang the bundles or individual flowers upside down in a warm, well-ventilated place out of direct sunlight. Depending on conditions, it usually takes about 2 to 3 weeks for the plants to dry completely. You'll be able to tell that a flower is completely dry when the stems snap easily. Before arranging the flowers, spray them with hair spray, an aerosol floral sealer, or clear lacquer to help prevent shedding and shattering. This technique is especially effective on ornamental grasses. If necessary, use thin floral wires (found in craft stores) to strengthen the stems.

OPPOSITE, CLOCKWISE FROM ABOVE RIGHT *'Strawberry Fields' gomphrena, crested celosia (*Celosia argentea *var.* cristata*), and pink statice (*Limonium sinuate*) are long-lasting flowers that hold their shape and color when cut. Arrangements with fresh and dried plants are fun to put together; here I've combined dried okra, rose hips, Mexican sage, hydrangeas, 'Indigo Spires' salvia, orange dahlias, and pink roses.*

dried flower topiary

Here's a fun twist on displaying dried flowers. For this project, use flowers you dry from your garden or pick some up at a craft store while you are gathering the other supplies. The material list is for making one topiary, but you might consider doubling it and creating two topiaries to place on top of a buffet or entrance table.

materials

- (1) 6-inch terra-cotta pot
- (1) 6-inch plastic foam ball
- (3) twigs about 21 inches long, bundled
- Duct tape
- Plaster of Paris
- Disposable container to mix plaster of Paris
- Hot glue gun
- Hot glue sticks
- Floral U-pins
- Jute twine
- Dried flowers (I used cockscomb celosia, 'Purple Flamingo' wheat celosia, sunflowers, bittersweet, 'Strawberry Fields' gomphrena, Mexican sage, and maple leaves)
- Sheet moss
- Scissors

1. To create the form, start with the terra-cotta pot and cover the drainage hole with duct tape.

2. Mix the plaster of Paris according to package directions. Place the bundle of twigs in the center of the pot to form the "trunk" of the topiary and pour plaster up to roughly ½ inch from the top of the container. Hold the twigs in place until the plaster sets, about 2 to 3 minutes. Then allow the plaster to dry, which takes approximately 30 minutes depending on the humidity. After the plaster hardens, trim the trunk from the top so that it rises 16 inches above the plaster of Paris base.

3. To prepare the foam ball so that it will easily slide on the trunk after it has been decorated with flowers, press it about 4 inches onto the end of the trunk. Pull it back off the trunk to begin adding dried flowers.

4. Now begin arranging dried blooms onto the foam ball. Start with larger flower sizes to create visual impact and use medium to small blooms to fill in and soften the arrangement. Larger flowers such as sunflowers can be attached to the foam ball with hot glue, while bundles of smaller flowers can be attached with floral U-pins.

5. When the ball is decorated, attach it to the trunk by putting hot glue in the hole and sliding the ball onto the trunk to anchor it in place. You could add finishing touches such as wrapping bittersweet or similar vines around the trunk, secured with hot glue, and concealing the plaster base with sheet moss and hot glue.

tips for dried flower arrangements

- If you are arranging dried flowers in containers, keep the stems tied together in bundles with string or rubber bands to create a stronger visual impact.
- Since dried flowers don't have to be watered, just about anything can serve as a container.
- Using a block of floral foam, begin by arranging the tall and spiky plants, placing them in the center of the composition and working out from there. Then select flowers that are round and bold to contrast the spikes. As you work from the center to the edge of the arrangement, use stems that you've progressively cut shorter. Now it's just a matter of filling in all of the spaces that are left.
- Apply essential oils of herbs, such as lavender, on the petals to give your arrangement a wonderful aroma.

Renewed Interest

Late summer and early fall are great times to visit all my favorite garden centers and nurseries to shop for end-of-the-season bargains. Many summer annuals are still available at rock-bottom prices, and nurseries often discount their perennials, shrubs, and trees to clear out their inventories. It's the perfect time to pick up plants to rejuvenate my summer containers that by now are looking a bit bedraggled. I'm on the hunt for plants that will put on a good show until frost, as well as those that can tolerate a light freeze. Before I head out to the nursery, I take one quick trip around the garden to evaluate my containers and decide which plants are past their prime and which ones are keepers. Once I've made my inspection, I create a list of how many plants I'll need to refresh the pots and then I'm ready to go.

FALL PERFORMERS

Asters (family Asteraceae)
Autumn fern (*Dryopteris erythrosora*)
Black-eyed Susan (*Rudbeckia* spp.)
'Blue Bird' nemesia (*Nemesia caerulea* 'Blue Bird')
Chrysanthemums (*Chrysanthemum* spp.)
Coral bells (*Heuchera* 'Dolce')
Dinosaur kale (*Brassica oleracea* 'Lacinato')
'Fireworks' goldenrod (*Solidago rugosa*)
'Goldilocks' lysimachia (*Lysimachia numulleria* 'Aurea')
Ivy (*Hedera* spp.)
Ornamental grasses
Ornamental peppers (*Capsicum annum*)
Pansies (*Viola* spp.)
Parsley (*Petroselinum crispum*)
Purple cabbage (*Brassica oleracea*)
'Superbells' calibrachoa (*Calibrachoa* 'Superbells')
Twinspur (*Diascia* spp.)
Salvias (*Salvia* spp.)
Sedums (*Sedum* spp.)
'Symphony' osteospermum (*Osteospermum* 'Symphony')
Toad lily (*Tricyrtis* spp.)

Once I've made my selections at the garden center and bring the plants home, I harvest the still-vibrant summer plants from their containers. I could just pull out the tired plants and try to shoehorn in new ones, but I've found that it's easier to gently remove the healthy summer plants I want to save, keeping as much of the root ball intact as possible, and transplant them to new containers. This gives me a chance to bring in some new seasonal containers with fresh soil, and it also offers me the opportunity to move around and recombine the summer plants.

I always follow my "three-shape rule" when choosing which plants to recombine in the new containers. I look for three plant forms—tall and spiky, round and full, trailing or cascading—when arranging new combinations. These forms complement one another well and create an appealing design. The ornamental grasses are often good choices to use for the tall and spiky element. Asters, chrysanthemums, and ornamental kale all have round and full forms that help to fill out the center of the display. Ivy, summer torenias, and sweet potato vines spill over the edge with their cascading habits, softening the look of the display. I look for these forms in both the summer and the fall plants. Once I've gotten my summer plants resituated and the fall plants tucked in beside them, I fill in with more soil and water the container well. As a last touch, I like to take a little time to weave the summer plants in with their new container-mates. This helps blend the lines between the plants and gives the container a more mature, grown-in look.

At the end of the season, before the ground freezes, you can transplant the new fall perennials into your garden's flower borders so you can continue to enjoy them next year.

OPPOSITE *The orange-red leaves of 'Texas Parking Lot' coleus play off the hues of 'Angelface Blue' angelonia, 'Religious Radish' coleus, cordyline, 'Superbells Pink' calibrachoa, 'Purple Lady' iresine, and 'Butterfly Pink' pentas, creating a rich and colorful autumnal composition.*

RIGHT *Wild and unruly, this container of white geraniums, 'Limelight' coleus, 'Diamond Frost' euphorbia, 'Angelina' sedum, and 'Mahogany' ajuga has seen its best days.* **BELOW** *The plants are spruced up and replanted with new companions: 'Vanilla Butterfly' argyranthemum and 'Helena's Blush' euphorbia. To cheer up the composition a bit more, the sedum is moved to its own container along with companion pots of 'Dolce Crème Brûlée' heuchera and 'Toffee Twist' sedge.*

before

after

RIGHT *This large container has been the summertime home of several plants, including variegated ribbon grass, 'Powis Castle' artemisia, 'Diamond Frost' euphorbia, blue lobelia, and purple petunias that had their heyday in spring and early summer.* **ABOVE** *With some pruning, the artemisia and 'Diamond Frost' euphorbia are well-behaved companions with 'Red Ruffles' coleus, 'Tricolor' sage, pink trailing snapdragons, and 'Sunsatia Raspberry' nemesia. Accenting pots of 'Tricolor' sage and 'Red Peacock' kale spark up the composition. The perennial ribbon grass found a new home in the garden.*

Turning Up the Color

By mid-September, the fall equinox—the day when the minutes of daylight and darkness are the same—has almost arrived. My northern gardening friends are awaiting their first frost, but here in my Zone 7 garden, with a hard freeze more than a month away, it is the faltering light that is most apparent to me. The days when I could work in the garden until 8:00 or 9:00 P.M. are just a memory. The sun sinks behind my neighbor's house by 6:00 P.M. and soon after I need to turn on a light to work outside. Even during the day I notice the light doesn't have the same brightness as it did during the summer. I find myself responding to this ever diminishing light by searching for plants that will embolden the garden with big, bright splashes of color.

I can always rely on goldenrod and asters to give me plenty of late-summer blooms, but to make sure that I have a big wash of vivid color deep into the autumn, I plant lots of garden mums (*Chrysanthemum* x *morifolium*). They just seem to be naturals for the fall landscape.

Some gardeners prefer to plant chrysanthemums in flower beds in the spring and grow them as perennials. As they develop, their summer foliage is bright green and grows quietly, letting summer flowers take center stage. Then, in autumn, the buds pop open in glorious hues and add their magic to fall borders. Other gardeners, especially those with smaller spaces, prefer to buy potted plants in early fall and drop them into borders just before they flower. I also like to wait until fall to add mums to my borders. Since I'm always trying to pack in as many plants as possible, bed space is at a premium, and rather than give up spots to grow mums as perennials, it works better for me to add them later in the season to replace a summer plant.

OPPOSITE *Fall is the time to pull out all the stops and fill the border with lots of color. Mexican sage, 'Indigo Spires' salvia, 'Powis Castle' artemisia, 'All Around Purple' gomphrena, 'Molten Lava' coleus, purple cabbage, 'Morning Light' miscanthus, 'Raspberry Parfait' dianthus, purple perilla, 'Bold Felicia' mums, and 'Patricia Ballard' asters put on a dazzling display.*

When I buy chrysanthemums at the garden center, I always look for healthy plants that are covered with buds and pass by those that are already in flower. In the bud state the mums have more of an opportunity to take root in the garden and fill out naturally in the landscape. They also bloom for a longer period of time. I likewise pass up any mums that look withered and dry. For all the buds to mature into flowers, it's important to keep them watered. Without plenty of moisture, the flowers can be small and malformed.

When placing them in the borders, I group several plants together to get the most visual impact and to create some drama. I also find that they appear more striking when the collection is a single color or closely related colors such as a light, medium, and darker shade of the same color.

Look around your yard to see what colors would best complement the existing landscape. If you decorate for fall with pumpkins and gourds, choose orange, bronze, yellow, and creamy white mums. If you have a lot of evergreen plants that provide a backdrop of varying shades of green foliage, try bright pinks, lavenders, pure whites, or reds. With such bold colors, a large grouping of mums can excite even the drabbest fall landscapes.

HOW TO CHOOSE AND CARE FOR MUMS

- Select disease-free plants with healthy, green foliage.
- To extend bloom time, pick plants with tight buds rather than opened flowers. More buds now mean more flowers later.
- Keep mums well watered. Potted mums dry out quickly and, if underwatered, will produce malformed flowers. For borders, water frequently the first two weeks until established.

Designer Mums

Much like the new fall fashions, each year plant breeders roll out the latest line of exciting chrysanthemums for gardeners to try on for size. With so many colors and varieties to choose from, mums make fall decorating easy. And with nearly a dozen flower forms to pick among, you can buy mums that look like pastel daisies, fluffy quilled zinnias, refined dahlias, or large, fancy flowers with incurving petals often called "football" mums. The chrysanthemum palette includes every color but blue, and the holding time for blossoms, even in a vase, is measured in weeks rather than days. Mums also thrive in the cool temperatures of fall. No wonder they're such a popular autumn plant.

There are lots of ways to use mums in your fall decoration. A quick way to create a friendly welcome at your front door is to fill baskets or containers with mums and mix in seasonal accents. I use a big rustic twig planter on my front porch this way. As a time saver, rather than repot the containers, I simply drop in the nursery pots of mums along with a frilly kale and ornamental pepper and conceal the tops with sheet moss. Who's to know? To give it more interest, I pile an assortment of gourds and pumpkins around the basket. In just minutes I have a colorful accent to greet my guests.

I find mums to be multipurpose decorating plants. They look equally at home in either casual arrangements or more formal settings. When planted in an elegant black iron urn, mums add just the right touch of buttoned-up sophistication; grouped together in a low basket, they are a focal point along a path. I also find them to be the perfect "round and full" form for my three-shape rule of designing containers, so I use them in planted pots with tall spiky grasses and cascading ivies as well as in hanging baskets.

As I begin to put together my autumn decorations, I notice that the leaves in the trees are starting to change color. Soon the canopy will be awash in an explosion of hues in reds, golds, and yellows.

RIGHT *Mums take on stately airs when presented in classic urns. Aptly named 'Debonair' chrysanthemums combine with 'Dynasty Pink' kale, 'Ramblin Plum' coleus, and 'Aureola' hakone grass.* **BELOW LEFT** *This twig plant stand is lined with sphagnum moss, concealing the plastic nursery pots that hold the mum, ornamental peppers and ruffled kale.* **BELOW RIGHT** *A rustic basket holds two violet-pink mums still in their plastic nursery pots. The bittersweet berries and red maple leaves soften the edge of the basket and hide the pots.* **OPPOSITE, LEFT** *Abundance, one of the twelve principles of design I follow in my gardens, is particularly important in autumn, so I load up on lots of mums.* **OPPOSITE, RIGHT** *A blank wall or fence is the perfect place to hang a trellised window box full of autumn plants.*

preserving leaves

When designing my fall arrangements, I always like to add some colorful fall leaves to the display. The texture and colors of the leaves serve as a nice contrast to soft plumes of ornamental grasses, colorful fall blooms, and seasonal accents such as berries and pumpkins. But if you've ever tried using leaves in decorating, you know that they quickly turn brittle and need to be replaced. I've found that using glycerin to preserve leaves solves the problem. The leaves take up the glycerin in place of water and remain pliable and easy to arrange. Many kinds of leaves can be preserved this way, including foliage from trees such as magnolia, dogwood, pear, beech, sycamore, plum, and poplar. Branches from shrubs such as barberry, forsythia, hydrangea, privet, rhododendron, and rose respond well to this process, too. Even leaves of many perennial herbaceous plants, including canna, coral bells (*Heuchera* spp.), sea holly (*Eryngium*), baby's breath (*Gypsophila*), and ivy (*Hedera*) are good candidates. I've had the best results with leaves from mature plants harvested in early autumn. Young, tender foliage tends to droop. Select only perfect specimens and wash the foliage with water to remove dirt or spray residue.

materials

Measuring cups
1-quart wide-mouthed Mason jar
Floral pruners
Glycerin (can be purchased at drugstores)
Mature foliage collected from the garden and well hydrated in water

1. Pour 2 cups of water into a small saucepan and heat the water to very hot but not boiling. Pour the hot water into the Mason jar—the solution should fill at least 3 inches of the jar. Add 1 cup of glycerin to the water in the jar. Stir vigorously to mix the glycerin with the hot water.

continues on following pages

of Man
GARDEN
AGE

2. If the plant material has woody stems, cut off the last inch with a slanting cut before starting the treatment.

3. Add the stems to the solution, but avoid getting foliage into the liquid. Set the jar aside in a dark room for several days. The leaves will change color as the solution is absorbed. Allow the stems to remain in the solution until the color is uniform to the edge of the leaf. This indicates that the absorption is complete. Good air circulation and warm weather will speed up the absorption. Wipe the leaves occasionally with a cloth dampened with the solution. This will help prevent drying before the glycerin reaches the edge of the leaves. The leaves may wilt if left in the solution too long. If this occurs, take them out of the jar, wipe them off, and hang them upside down to dry.

4. Store preserved plant materials in labeled boxes to protect them from damage and dirt until use. Before storage, wipe the leaves carefully with a soft cloth to remove excess moisture. Check the boxes frequently during the first few weeks to be sure there is no leakage from the leaves, which might cause mold.

5. When you are ready to use the leaves for decorations, remove them from the boxes and combine with other seasonal materials, such as bittersweet, ornamental grasses, seed pods, and berries. The leaves also make stunning arrangements on their own when displayed in vases. While glycerin will not preserve the color of the foliage, the leaves will remain pliable and have a waxy, shiny appearance. If done correctly, foliage preserved this way can be cleaned and returned to their storage boxes and will last indefinitely.

Wrapping Things Up

Soon enough, nighttime temperatures will dip into the 30s. As in spring, it is hard to predict when a freeze might arrive. I've found that it usually comes on a still, cloudless night. But it's always a good idea to get ready. For years I used lightweight sheets to cover plants in the flower borders and in my vegetable garden, but recently I've tried frost blankets with good results. The blankets are made of polypropylene, so they are lightweight and strong, and since they let in both rain and sunlight, you can leave them on all day without fear of baking the frost-tender plants. When weighted down on all sides, they trap the soil's warmth and keep out the cold. I've put my blankets through all kinds of abuse and they've held up just fine. Frost blankets are available in different weights; the heavier the weight, the longer trapped heat will remain under the blanket. Medium (4-ounce) blankets protect crops to 28 degrees F, while 6-ounce heavyweight blankets will protect woody ornamental crops to a temperature of 0 degrees. You can even enhance the protection by sprinkling water over the top of the blanket when temperatures reach freezing, which creates an igloo effect over the ground. One thing

I've discovered is that they are cozy enough to attract cats. One morning I found my garden cat, Marge, snuggled comfortably under the blanket.

Another way I lengthen my vegetable garden's growing season is by topping off some of the raised beds with mini greenhouses. To create the frame I bend an 8-foot piece of wire fencing over the top of my 4 x 4-foot wood-framed bed. This creates a U-shaped form over the bed. When cold weather threatens, I simply drape a piece of heavy plastic (or frost blankets) over the top, covering all sides, and weight it down. This captures enough heat that my vegetables stay toasty through the night. You can do the same thing over any section of your garden by securing the ends of the fencing into the ground with wooden stakes.

With all my frost preparations in place, I can breathe a little easier. I know I can't keep the cold away from my plants forever, but it may buy me a little extra time. Now I can take a deep breath and enjoy adding more autumnal decorations to the outside of my home.

ESTIMATED FIRST FROST DATES BY ZONE

- Zone 3: September 1st–30th
- Zone 4: September 1st–30th
- Zone 5: September 30th–October 30th
- Zone 6: September 30th–October 30th
- Zone 7: October 15th–November 15th
- Zone 8: October 30th–November 30th
- Zone 9: November 30th–December 30th
- Zone 10: November 30th–December 30th
- Zone 11: Frost-free

Pumpkins

Pumpkins are a particular fall favorite of mine. They're a stylish and simple way to decorate for autumn, and there is just something about their shape and feel that epitomizes the fruitfulness of the season. Every year I purchase a wheelbarrowful of varying shapes, sizes, and colors to dress up my home and garden.

I like to stagger pumpkins down the steps of my front porch along with a few brightly colored mums or fill a rustic twig basket with green gourds, orange pumpkins, and purple kale to set on my kitchen countertop. It's easy to make a pumpkin topiary by stacking a variety of squatty, flat-bottomed pumpkins on top of one another. I have even cut slices across the top of miniature pumpkins and used them as place card holders for dinner parties. Pumpkins also make excellent containers for fall flower arrangements. Just hollow them out and place a container inside to hold the water for the flowers.

BELOW *Guests enter the garden with a smile when they see this casual collection of pumpkins piled up around the gate that leads to my front door.* OPPOSITE *Cool temperatures bring out the flavors of fall-planted lettuce greens and vegetables. Plastic-covered wire-framed hoops protect the plants from frosty nights and extend my growing season by several weeks.*

CLOCKWISE FROM ABOVE LEFT *Place a low, flat-bottomed vase inside a hollowed-out pumpkin and fill the vase with water and a selection of colorful flowers, leaves, and berries. Fashion a name place holder for your autumn table by cutting a wide slit on the top of a mini pumpkin and slipping the tag inside. Stack graduated sizes of flat-bottomed pumpkins on top of one another to create a topiary; remove the stems from all but the top pumpkin and stabilize the tower by applying some heavy-duty adhesive such as Liquid Nails between them.* **OPPOSITE** *Fill a window box with a collection of pumpkins, gourds, and Osage orange balls, and then accent the display with fruited bittersweet branches.*

cinderella's centerpiece

Pumpkins and roses—now, that's a combination you don't see every day. I couldn't resist the challenge of seeing what I could come up with by putting those two unlikely companions together in an arrangement. I needed a centerpiece for a fairly formal dinner party and the results seem to be just what I was looking for. With the pumpkin sitting on a floral foam ring, all it took was a few minutes to push the stems of the peach-colored roses, leaves, and bittersweet in the foam. If you use a pedestal as I did, make sure the pumpkin is wider than it is tall so it doesn't block the view across the table.

materials

Squatty-type pumpkin
Floral foam ring, 10 inches in diameter
Shallow bowl
Wooden or glass pedestal
Pruners
A dozen peach roses, bittersweet, fall leaves

1. Soak the floral foam ring in water overnight.

2. Place the ring on the pedestal. If the pedestal is not waterproof, put the ring on a plastic liner, as I did, or in a shallow bowl.

3. Put the pumpkin on top of the floral foam ring.

4. Cut the stems of the roses to about 4 inches and insert them into the foam to create a circle of flowers around the base of the pumpkin.

5. Add colorful leaves and bittersweet to fill out the display.

more pumpkin tips

- Cover cut areas of the pumpkin as well as the inside with petroleum jelly to keep them fresh longer.
- Instead of a candle use a battery-powered lamp—it's safer.
- If you do use a candle, rub the inside of the pumpkin with cinnamon, nutmeg, or other spices so that as the rind heats it will emit a pleasant fragrance.
- Pumpkins make good soil conditioners, so don't just throw them out. Cut them up and toss them in the compost corral (see how to build a corral on page 156).

apple-tasting party

What's fall without a fresh, crisp apple? In my family it was an autumn ritual to go to the apple orchard and get several bushel basketfuls of apples to keep on our unheated porch. Anytime we wanted a snack, it was there within our reach.

Over the past several years, I've become interested in the varieties of apples that were planted years ago. My curiosity was sparked at a dinner with friends in England. We finished the meal by passing around trays of several different varieties of sliced apples. The host shared stories of the apples' pedigree, making the enjoyment of the fruits even sweeter. One variety that we sampled was 'Cox's Orange Pippin', an apple that originated in England in 1825 from random seed stock. The spicy, nutty, and pearlike flavor of its cream-colored flesh was incredibly delicious. I can still remember its flavor.

When I returned home I began looking for other types of apples grown in the 1800s in this country and found that it was difficult to find any beyond the familiar standbys like Granny Smith and Red Delicious. A little research revealed that in the late 1800s there were more than 700 apple varieties that were available from commercial nurseries. Today there are fewer than 50. Many wonderful varieties are believed to be extinct. Four of the hundreds of documented varieties that can no longer be found are the Arkansas Beauty, the Chattahoochee, the Red Banana, and the Tuscaloosa (which won the premium prize at the 1858 Montgomery, Alabama, fair). Luckily, some individuals have taken it upon themselves to maintain a large number of apple varieties and offer trees and their fruits for sale.

Although I don't have a lot of room to grow apples in my garden, it doesn't keep me from experiencing many of these delicious varieties grown by our forebearers. Each fall I order a few boxes of heirloom apples through the mail and host my own version of an apple-tasting party. Wine, cheese, and sliced apples are sampled along with stories about the varieties' colorful past. For my casual sit-down party, I invited five friends over to sample twelve different types. Each apple was sliced and passed around while I shared some of the history about the fruit. Guests had scorecards to judge which apple was their favorite. To cleanse the palate between samples, we also nibbled on fresh-baked French bread and butter, cheese, and walnuts.

continues on following page

Pitmaston Pineapple
Kandil Sinap

gather the apples

To begin planning your tasting party, find out if there are local growers in your area. Your county extension service might be able to help you with that information, or you can visit your local farmers' market. If a local source isn't available, order a sampler box of apples from a mail-order company (see Source Guide, page 209). For a group of six people, plan to sample around twelve varieties of apples at the party.

before guests arrive

- Make a place card label for each apple variety.
- Prepare a short description of each apple. Stories about its history and use are always of interest.
- Provide a 4 x 6-inch index card for each guest to use as a scorecard, with columns for variety name, score, and comments.
- Set the table with a dinner plate, a sharp fruit knife or paring knife, a pencil, and a scorecard for each guest.
- Set out several wooden bowls for collecting the cores and peelings and arrange cutting boards of cheese, baskets of bread and butter, and bowls of walnuts.

once guests are seated

- Take the first apple and divide it in six slices, one for each guest.
- Leave the slices intact with core and peel and pass them on a plate.
- As the apple is passed around, read the description.
- Give everyone a chance to sample and discuss the flavor.
- Repeat until all the apples have been sampled.
- You can either gather the cards and compile the scores or tally the score as a group once the sampling is complete.

You may also want to ask your guests to bring copies of their favorite apple recipe. At the end of the party, guests can take them home as a keepsake.

GREAT BAKING APPLES

- **Arkansas Black** Sharp flavor and aromatic.
- **Baldwin** A nice blend of sweet and tart.
- **Empire** Slightly tart, all-purpose apple.
- **Golden Delicious** Mellow and sweet.
- **Ida Red** Tangy and tart; keeps its shape in baking.
- **Jonathan** Moderately tart and a bit spicy.
- **Rome Beauty** Richly flavored; holds its shape well.
- **York** Firm, crisp, and winelike flavor.

apple cranberry cake

This recipe has all the flavors of fall. It makes a delicious fruitcake-like snack that is great with afternoon coffee. I use baking apples that have a good balance of sweet and tart flavors. Look for those with flesh that is dense, so they won't give off too much water as they cook.

INGREDIENTS

¾ cup butter at room temperature, cut into small pieces
¾ cup light brown sugar
3 eggs
2 cups whole wheat flour
1 cup white flour
1 teaspoon baking powder
2 teaspoons pumpkin pie spice
1½ cups baking apples, peeled, cored, and diced
1 cup dried cranberries (soaked in hot water for ½ hour and drained)
5 tablespoons milk
2 tablespoons chopped walnuts
2 tablespoons sugar

1. Preheat oven to 325 degrees F. Lightly grease and flour a deep, 8-inch round cake pan.

2. In a medium mixing bowl, cream together the butter, brown sugar, and eggs. Avoid overbeating. In another medium bowl, sift together all the dry ingredients: whole wheat and white flours, baking powder, and pumpkin pie spice. Mix thoroughly and then add to the creamed mixture.

3. Fold in the apples, cranberries, and enough milk to soften the mixture. Spoon the mixture into the cake pan and level the surface. Sprinkle the top with chopped walnuts and sugar. Bake for 1 hour 30 minutes, until golden brown and firm to the touch. Cool in the pan for 15 minutes or so, then turn out on a wire rack to cool completely. Cut into wedge-shaped slices. Serves 12.

gourd garland

While it's always rewarding to grow food and flowers, I must confess a weakness for a plant that I grow just for fun. Each year, I try to make room in my garden for a few gourds. I love all their odd shapes and wacky markings, and have a particular fondness for the hard-shelled gourds that last for years. They make great additions to my fall projects.

Along with saving my tomatoes, at the first sign of frost I also gather up my gourds to preserve some for fall decorations. Even if you didn't grow any for yourself, you can find them at craft stores, farmers' markets, even grocery stores. Here are a few things you may find helpful if you'd like to save some for your projects.

1. Gourds should be completely dry. You can do this simply by air-drying them in a well-ventilated area such as a garage, basement, carport, or shed. You may find that crust and mold appear on them as they dry. This is normal. Just wash them in warm soapy water with a steel wool pad to remove the residue.

2. Once they are clean, wipe them with a cloth and let them dry thoroughly. Large gourds might need a light sanding with fine sandpaper before the next step, which can be painting, varnishing, or waxing.

3. I like to bring out the natural tones of large gourds. What works for me and gives them a nice shine is just an ordinary paste wax.

4. I prefer to paint the smaller gourds. But I always dip them in varnish first. This keeps the paint from being completely absorbed. Dried gourds can have a really great look in a simple glass bowl or basket.

Once you've preserved your gourds, you can have fun using them to create all kinds of fall displays. I find this dramatic gourd presentation to be one of the simplest to create. It's eye-catching hung near a door, and when combined with other colorful plants and seasonal accents, it makes a beautiful embellishment for an entry. I guarantee you'll get lots of comments!

materials

Approximately 25 medium to large gourds, cleaned and, if desired, polished with paste wax (the varieties used here were Birdhouse, Dipper, and Corsican)

Garden twine

Scissors

1. Decide where your garland will hang and cut the twine to the desired length for the finished garland. I used about 6 feet for my garland.

2. Cut smaller individual pieces of twine and tie them around the stem of each gourd.

3. Use the twine tied to the individual gourds to attach them to the garland length of twine. Add gourds every few inches.

4. Hang the garland in the desired location and fill in any gaps by adding more gourds. If you want to hang the gourds vertically, rather than attach each gourd to one piece of twine, cut a number of individual twine pieces to different lengths and hang the gourds at staggered heights for an interesting effect.

Palmolive

SIGNATURE PLANT

1. Japanese Silver Grass
2. Fountain grass and sedum 'Autumn Joy'
3. Switchgrass 'Heavy Metal'
4. Pink muhly grass
5. Mexican Feather Grass
6. Feather reed grass 'Karl Foerster'
7. 'Morning Light'
8. Purple fountain grass 'Rubrum'
9. Black fountain grass 'Moudry'

Ornamental Grasses

In the late days of fall, ornamental grasses are standouts in the garden. Many varieties develop feathery seed heads that dance and wave in the wind, lending textural beauty and movement to a garden's design. These grasses are forgiving about soil and, once established, very drought tolerant, making them ideal for growing in areas where water is limited. The first time I planted an ornamental grass, I was skeptical. As you can imagine, after years of pulling grass from my flower beds, the irony was almost too much. I combined dwarf fountain grass (*Pennisetum alopecuroides* 'Hameln') with black-eyed Susan (*Rudbeckia fulgida*) and 'Autumn Joy' sedum (*Sedum spectabile*) and the result was a beautiful composition for late summer. Since then, I have found many ways to use grasses in my garden designs.

1.
2.
3.
4.
5.
6.
7.
8.
9.

planting ahead

When I discovered that a close friend's favorite flower was the peony, I wanted to do something special for her, so I designed a 14-foot-diameter circular bed and packed it with all the soft pink varieties of peonies that she loved. Now we can anticipate the display every spring and have a special celebration to enjoy the show. The design gave her plenty of blooms so she could cut armloads of flowers to bring indoors without diminishing the presentation.

You can adapt my design by scaling it up or down to fit the area you have.

materials

25-foot measuring tape
Surveying spray paint
Package of plastic flags on wires
Long nails
Wooden measuring rod (or yardstick)
Spade
Rototiller
Soil amendments such as sand, compost, and manure (depending on your soil type)
Slow-release fertilizer
(12) peony tubers (for a 14-foot-diameter bed)
(28) 1-gallon containerized boxwoods (I used *Buxus* 'Green Velvet')
Bucket

1. Select an open, well-drained spot that gets at least 6 hours of direct sun a day.

2. To draw out the circle:

- Determine the center point of the bed and drive a nail through the metal loop at the end of a measuring tape.
- Extend the tape out 7 feet. Place a flag at that point.
- With the tape still extended 7 feet, move around the circumference 3 feet to the right of the first flag and place another flag 7 feet from the center. Continue moving around the perimeter, flagging points in 3-foot increments to outline the circle.

3. Once the circle is flagged, spray-paint a line on the ground between the flags to clearly define the border.

4. With a spade, cut around the edge of the circle about 2 to 3 inches deep. Cut a parallel line approximately 2 feet toward the center. Skin back sections of the sod between the lines and remove. Continue cutting and removing the sod until the circle is free of grass. (Tip: Lay sheets of plastic next to the circle to hold the pieces of sod, making it easier to remove from the lawn. The sod can be used to fill in low places in other areas of your yard.)

5. Peonies do best in rich, well-drained soil. If your soil needs amendments, add sand (for increased drainage), compost, and packaged manure. For my clay-based soil, I use a 1:1 ratio—1 part garden soil, 1 part sand, 1 part manure, and 1 part compost. Rototill the amendments into the soil. Till the beds to a depth of 18 inches.

continues on following pages

Often, instead of a looking at a calendar or a watch, I use natural events in the garden to tell me when it's time to do certain things. For instance, in summer, the perfect time to weed is after a long soaking rain; in early fall, the best time to transplant perennials is on an overcast, windless day. In that same way, when the leaves begin to fall in late autumn, I know it's time to plant peony tubers.

6. Consider the mature size of the boxwoods as you position them equally around the edge of the circle. 'Green Velvet' boxwood is a slow-growing hybrid variety that matures to 4 feet by 4 feet, so I space the shrubs about 30 inches apart (measuring from the center of each plant). Once you are satisfied with their arrangement, plant them around the circumference.

7. Using a measuring rod, flag the position for the tubers 30 inches apart throughout the bed. I interspersed two varieties, 'Festiva Maxima' and 'Sarah Bernhardt'. Air circulation between the plants is important, so you may need to adjust spacing depending on the variety you choose. For maximum impact, you may want to select varieties that bloom at the same time, or mix together early-, mid-, and late-season peonies to keep the color coming for a longer period of time.

8. Dig a hole for each tuber and sprinkle in a handful of slow-release fertilizer. Now here's the important part! Plant the tubers with the "eyes" (growth buds) pointing up under no more than 1 inch of soil in mild-winter climates, and 2 inches in cold climates. Trust me, if you plant them too deep, you will have foliage but no flowers. Since the soil is loose, hold the tubers at the appropriate depth, add water to settle the ground and remove air pockets, cover with a little soil, water again, and add more soil. Adjust the depth of the tuber as needed in case the soil settles below the optimum planting depth.

9. Optional: Place a garden ornament in the center of the bed to give it a finished look.

10. Two inches of winter mulch is necessary for all peonies the first year to prevent frost-heaving. When you see some tips emerge in the spring, remove the mulch.

Thinking of Spring

On most days now, there's a wintry bite to the wind, but although the air might be nippy, the ground is still warm and welcomes the frequent showers that roll through. The wet soil and fallen leaves combine to create a rich, earthy smell that is unmistakably autumn. Before I can let the season go, I have to get some bulbs in the ground.

I've been planting bulbs in the fall as far back as I can remember. It's a ritual that is just as much a part of my autumn traditions as Thanksgiving. In fact, that's usually about the time I plant my spring-flowering bulbs. I often wait until after the first frost, so I can clean up my garden and have a better look at where I want to plant them.

In my part of the world where the winters are relatively mild, tulips are treated as annuals. Nearly all hybrid tulips need an extended period of winter chill to bloom well. This is a problem for most gardeners in the lower, coastal, and tropical South. They must refrigerate tulip bulbs for 8 to 10 weeks prior to planting (see "Precooling Bulbs," right). If I get my bulbs in the ground around Thanksgiving, that gives them enough chill to bloom in the spring, but they don't normally repeat the following year. Daffodils are a different story. They are reliable perennials, so I don't have to plant as many of those each year. But I must admit, when I make my bulb order, I always see some new varieties I can't do without, so I plant those at the same time.

Bulb planting is something that I think everyone should try. It is one of the most no-fail recipes I know. There is really nothing to it because the flower is already packaged inside the bulb and all you have to do is coax it out by planting it properly. When I plant tulips in my garden, I dig out an area the size of the drift of blooms I want. A good rule of thumb for the depth is to cover them three times the height of the bulb, and I always work in good, rich compost and bonemeal before placing the bulbs approximately 6 to 8 inches apart.

PRECOOLING BULBS

I'm often asked if spring-flowering bulbs need to be precooled before planting. If you're planting daffodils, they don't require any chilling to bloom. Just keep them in a cool, dry place out of the sun and don't let them freeze. They can be planted anywhere in the country. I've planted daffodils as early as the first of September and as late as January and they always seem to do just fine.

If you are planting tulips, hyacinths, and crocuses, they all need a period of chilling at about 40 to 45 degrees F for at least 6 to 8 weeks. If you live in a part of the country where winter temperatures fall below freezing, planting these in the autumn is really all they need. But if you live where winters are mild, you'll need to prechill your bulbs or buy them prechilled. If you want to do it yourself and you can spare the room, the easiest method is to store them in the refrigerator. Avoid storing the bulbs near ripening fruit, like apples, though. The fruit gives off ethylene gas, which can damage the tiny flower bud inside the bulbs.

When selecting bulbs, look for those that are fresh and healthy looking and very firm. And avoid those that have been frozen or dried and have soft spots or look withered. They're not worth the effort.

tulip trough

Planting tulips in containers is a great way to add a bright accent near a doorway or entrance to a garden path. It's ideal for those who have limited space. There's really nothing to it. All you need is a frost-proof container, a bag of potting soil, and a few bags of bulbs. For this project, I wanted to see just how many tulips I could get in one container. When I found this long metal trough, I knew I had the perfect container for my experiment. Look around your home and find a container that you'd like to display near an entry in spring. Coordinate the color of your bulbs with the container and the house. Come next spring you'll enjoy a spectacular display of blooms.

materials

Metal trough 10 inches wide by 2 feet long*
(2) 16-quart bags of potting soil
(1) small box of slow-release fertilizer
(75) 'Queen of the Night' tulips (or ones of your choice)

*It is important that you use a frost-proof container that won't crack in cold weather. I used a metal trough. Wood, resin, concrete, or plastic will also work.

1. Fill the container up to about 6 inches from the top with potting mix and add a handful of slow-release fertilizer to the soil.

2. Place the bulbs on top of the soil. I like to make a display that has a strong visual impact, so I position the bulbs shoulder to shoulder, or cheek to jowl as they say. The 'Queen of the Night' tulip bulbs I used produce dramatic large, velvety, deep black-maroon flowers that are borne on 2-foot-tall stems.

3. With the bulbs in place, cover them with 5 inches of potting soil, leaving roughly a 1-inch gap between the top of the soil and the rim of the container to keep water from spilling over.

4. Once the bulbs are planted, move the container to a shady, out-of-the-way place in the yard and water it. I keep it there all winter, checking on it occasionally to make sure the soil is moist but not soggy or the bulbs can rot. If you live in an area of the country where cold winters are the norm, you may need to store the container in the garage or shed to avoid damage from the cold. As spring arrives, move the trough out into a sunny location.

black gold for the garden

When I was in my teens, I usually tried to avoid the chore of raking the leaves, but since I discovered how valuable those leaves really are, my attitude has completely changed—now I look forward to it. Instead of seeing leaves strewn across my garden, I see piles of black gold before me. Decomposed organic material, or compost, is one of the best things you can add to improve your garden's soil. It is full of nutrients, builds soil structure, encourages beneficial soil life, and increases the soil's ability to hold water. There is really nothing better for your garden than compost and no better ingredient than leaves. Leaves are made from lots of complex chemicals that once broken down, plants eat up.

To make the most out of this great natural resource, I use a compost corral. Composting is simple: nature does all the work; all you need is a place for it to happen. This design is easy to put together with a minimum of materials.

materials

(16) 8-foot landscape timbers

(4) concrete blocks

(4) concrete reinforcing rods, ⅝ inch in diameter and 2 feet long

1. Begin by placing the four concrete blocks 8 feet apart (the same length as the timbers) to form a square. The blocks elevate the corral, so as the materials break down you can easily shovel the compost from the bottom.

2. Next drill a hole just halfway through two of the landscape timbers at each end, making sure the hole is slightly larger than the diameter of the rod. These will be the bottom rungs of the corral and will serve as a base for holding the concrete reinforcing rod. For the rest of the timbers, drill the hole all the way through.

3. Set the two "base" timbers on the concrete blocks with the holes facing up, and then span the ends of these with two more timbers to create a square. It is a similar process as when you built things out of Lincoln Logs.

4. Now align the holes in the top two timbers with the half holes in the bottom two timbers and insert the concrete reinforcing rods.

5. To complete the corral, just alternately stack the remaining timbers one on top of another over each rod. Stacking the timbers like this will create air spaces. And that's important for decomposition.

When it comes to composting, I've learned that there is a way you can layer the materials in the bin that will speed up the process. The only ingredients you need are organic materials such as fall leaves, grass clippings, and raw vegetable scraps from the kitchen, and water and oxygen.

The process works best if you layer green, nitrogen-rich clippings with brown, carbon-rich material such as the leaves at a ratio of about 1 part green to 1 part brown. The nitrogen helps speed up the decomposition of the leaves. You don't want to add sticks and branches, diseased plant material, or cooked food and weeds to the compost pile, as these items either take too long to break down, may spread unwanted pathogens in the compost, attract animals, or add weed seeds. When adding leaves to the compost bin, don't let them mat down in thick layers, because that would keep oxygen from helping break down the material. You can chop the leaves into smaller pieces by running a lawnmower over low piles. Water is also a key ingredient. Keeping the materials moist is like putting fuel on the fire. Lightly water and turn your compost about once every 2 weeks.

Even with the layering technique, the process takes time, generally about 6 months, but if you're in a hurry, you can accelerate it by adding a source of nitrogen such as granular commercial fertilizer or more grass clippings. To keep your compost going strong through the cold months, make sure the pile is at least 3 feet high and cover it with plastic to help hold in the heat.

Next spring, your efforts will be rewarded with wheelbarrow loads of compost that you can add to enrich your soil's fertility. It's performed miracles in my garden!

beeswax candles

When most of us think of bees, we are reminded of those industrious little workers that produce all of that sweet honey. Well, as much as I appreciate the honey, the thanks we really owe bees is for their work as pollinators. Without them we'd have none of our favorite foods such as apples, cucumbers, melons, and berries.

Making beeswax candles is an activity the whole family can enjoy. All you need are sheets of beeswax and wicks, available at craft stores, at beekeeping supply companies, or online. Craft stores carry kits with two 8 x 16-inch sheets of wax and accompanying wicks.

materials

Sheets of beeswax
Wicks

1. Start on a clean, flat surface or cover a table with kraft or waxed paper to help keep the beeswax clean. Lay out one sheet of wax and smooth the edges. If working conditions are cold, the wax may crack when rolled. It should be pliable but not soft. If need be, you can warm it up by placing it on a towel-lined cookie sheet in a low oven (250 degrees F) for a few minutes. These finished candles are 8 inches tall, the size of the sheet, so no cutting is necessary. To create shorter candles, cut the sheet to the desired height with a utility knife.

2. Cut the wick 1 inch longer than the height of the candle. Lay the wick about ⅛ inch from the edge of the wax, with the extra 1 inch of wick hanging over the top of the sheet, and press it down lightly. Carefully crimp the wax over the wick all the way down the edge, keeping the wick straight and in place.

3. Now gently roll the sheet tightly toward the other edge of the wax, making sure the top and bottom edges of the sheet are straight and even. Roll tightly but avoid bending or crushing the honeycomb surface.

4. When the candle is rolled to the end, gently press the edges into the coiled candle to seal the seam. For a tighter seal, dip a metal spatula in hot water to warm it and then press against the seam.

5. If a thicker candle is desired, you can increase the diameter by rolling the first sheet with the wick as described, and then line up the edge of a new sheet with the unsealed, outer edge of the candle. Begin to roll again until the desired diameter is reached. Two of the 8 x 16-inch sheets make a 2½-inch-wide pillar candle.

other tips

- I like to use the honeycombed wax, but you can find it in smooth sheets as well. Sheets are also available in a wide range of colors. The cost for an 8 x 16-inch sheet will run you about $2.
- Determine the size wick to purchase by the diameter of the candles you plan to make. Most sources will have a chart or recommendations to help you pick out the right wick. Wicks come in flat braid or square braid. For the most flexibility, you may want to purchase a range of wick sizes.
- Buy enough wax and wick that you will be able to do a few test runs.

horn of plenty

Thanksgiving marks the last big event in the fall season. Far and away, it's my favorite holiday because it combines all my favorite things—getting together with family and friends to dine on wonderful food and a daylong celebration centered on the bounty from the land. To get in the holiday spirit, I like to fill my house with lots of beautiful materials from the garden. I begin at the front door with a cornucopia overflowing with colorful flowers, gourds, corn, and grasses, to signify the wealth of the harvest.

materials

2 x 2-foot 1-inch mesh chicken wire
Hot glue gun and hot glue sticks
Sheet moss
Grapevine
Hair spray
Plants, cut flowers, fruits, and vegetables of the season
Floral tape
Floral foam
Floral sticks
8-inch papier-mâché container (or other lightweight holder)

1. Start by rolling the 2 x 2-foot piece of chicken wire diagonally from one corner to the other to create a cone. To hold it together bend the ends of the wire into the body and curve the closed end into the classic cornucopia shape. For the open end, just roll back the edges to form a lip. Be sure to make the opening large enough to hold an 8-inch container.

2. Slip the 8-inch papier-mâché container into the cornucopia. You can find these at most hobby stores, and they are usually white. I like to use them because they are so lightweight.

3. Next cover the wire form with sheet moss. Using a hot glue gun, attach sections of sheet moss to the frame. You may find that smaller pieces of moss are easiest to handle.

4. As a final touch, wrap the entire horn in grapevine. This gives it a nice accent and helps secure the moss. I've found that a light coating of hair spray or clear lacquer helps to keep the moss in place.

5. Now you are ready to really get creative and fill the horn of plenty with all sorts of things that symbolize the harvest season, such as dried fruits and vegetables as well as living plants like kale, mums, and ivy. Begin by placing floral foam in the container and push it toward the back to leave room in the front for other things. Then secure it with floral tape. Start at the back of the cornucopia with tall and spiky elements such as Russian sage or wheat or ornamental grass. Next add fullness with gourds, corn, and dried flowers. If you are planning to use live potted plants, remove them from their pots, shake off excess soil, moisten the roots, and slip the root ball in a plastic bag secured with a rubber band. This will help the plants last longer and they'll fit easier in the arrangement. Another trick I've learned is to spike gourds and small pumpkins with a floral stick and then simply push the stick into the floral foam. This keeps round objects in place. And finally, to cascade down the front, slip in a few ivy plants. Twist a wire loop on the back of the horn as a hanger to securely fasten it to the door.

thanksgiving tray

By Thanksgiving, Jack Frost has been nipping at the edges of my garden, but I find that nature still offers a wealth of beauty that can be gathered to create an eye-catching display. During late autumn a new palette of colors and textures emerges from the landscape to serve as a creative catalyst for seasonal decorations.

When I'm in the idea stage of making an arrangement, I like to brew a nice, steaming hot cup of coffee, slip on a jacket, and enjoy a walk around my garden to see what's available. What I'm looking for are items with interesting shapes and textures. The fun is to let the plan evolve depending on what I find. Once I have surveyed my surroundings and gathered the items I'd like to use, I'm ready to put the arrangement together.

materials

Tray

Waterproof liner, if needed

(3) pillar candles (I used cream-colored 3 x 7-inch wax candles)

(3) clear glass hurricane lamps

Gourds

Miniature pumpkins

Leaves

Floral vials

1. Arrange 3 pillar candles on the tray and slip hurricane lamps over them. Rather than lining them up, bring the middle candle slightly forward.

2. Since I already had some colorful gourds and miniature pumpkins left over from Halloween, I decided to use them in this arrangement. If you don't have any on hand, you can find them at a grocery or craft store. They are available in a variety of colors, shapes, and sizes.

3. Pile the pumpkins around the bases of the lamps and fit the gourds around the edges to fill in. Then add a second layer of gourds to build interest and dimension.

4. The leaves on my neighbor's Bradford pear had just turned a gorgeous shade of ruby red, and she was willing to share, so I gathered a handful to add to the display. Since leaves are often short-lived once they are picked, I slipped them into small water-filled floral vials to extend their freshness. The vials are easily camouflaged by tucking them among the pumpkins and gourds. If vials aren't available, you can simply replace any faded leaves with new ones as needed or dry them with glycerin following the steps on page 132. The leaves offer a layer of texture and brilliance to the arrangement, providing a soft and ephemeral contrast to the smooth, hard surfaces of the pumpkins and gourds.

5. As a finishing touch, add stems of dried bittersweet or other berried branches you may find. The vines provide another layer of interest to the arrangement, flowing in elegant lines above the static objects in the tray.

6. Make final adjustments and then place the tray on a side table or use it as the centerpiece at your next gathering. I find it soothing to see the warm glow of candlelight play off the colorful collection of objects in this autumnal display.

winter.

The event that kick-starts the winter season and firmly closes the door on autumn is the first hard freeze. Winter weather in my mid-South garden is about as unpredictable as a Sunday visit from my family. I can't be sure who will arrive first or what to expect once they get here. There have been days in December when my roses were still in bloom, while in other years the garden is covered in a blanket of snow in October. When freezing temperatures do come knocking at the door, my response is to jet outside and scurry around the garden like I'm being chased. In a way, I am. It's always a race against time until sundown. I lug containers of plants into the lathe house, hill mulch around prized perennials, gather up the last vegetables, and cut any remaining flowers.

The next morning, as I emerge from the back door the transformation is nothing less than amazing. During the slow, lingering days of autumn there is plenty of time to appreciate the garden's slow decline. The turn of the seasons between summer and fall seems more like a gentle tussle. Not so with winter. One night in the 20s and fall is unceremoniously kicked off the stage. The freeze puts a period at the end of the sentence that began last spring with "This year, my garden will be. . . ."

As the sun rises over the frosted plants and the last leaves let go, the garden reveals its bony frame. To keep the garden's design from disappearing with the cold, I've learned to strengthen its structure with several kinds of plants and objects that will retain their form all winter. The line and shape of hedges, buildings, and branches as well as varied textures, colorful barks, bright berries, and even subtle blooms add layers of visual interest to my winter landscape.

The hustle and bustle around the holidays pulls my attention away from the garden, but I still find ways to weave it into the fabric of my daily life. Now that I've finished potting up all my spring flowering bulbs outside, I take the activity inside by going through my cupboards and pulling out all the containers I can find to fill with paperwhite and amaryllis bulbs. Over the next few months, these easy-to-grow blooms fill my house with fragrance and flowers, adding life throughout the dark days of winter.

Another way I keep things in the garden lively is to throw a wildlife party in December. This new tradition is a low-stress alternative to a traditional holiday affair. The guests of honor at this celebration are the birds. Family and friends gather in the garden to decorate every surface they can find with all kinds of treats for our feathered friends. It's a delightful afternoon full of laughter and fun and, best of all, the birds enjoy their free buffet long after the party is over.

As the holidays draw near I enjoy harvesting berries and foliage from my garden to decorate the house. It is so satisfying to brew a hot drink, pull on a coat, and grab my hand pruners to walk around the yard and let the garden inspire my creations. Sprigs of boxwood, clusters of nandina berries, limbs from my needlepoint holly—all find their way into a festive centerpiece or winter window box design.

After the holidays, I'm often found inspecting flower beds and buds for signs of spring. When none are found, I satisfy myself by looking through seed catalogs and making plans for things I'll do once it warms up. By February, it's time to get back outside and prune up my roses and other trees and shrubs before the sap starts to rise. Spring's quickened pace is about to set in, so I savor the last quiet days of winter.

Enliven Your Winter Garden

Although it is tempting to add lots of holiday decorations at this time of year, I find that it saves me time and effort if I create accents with a broader appeal so they enhance the garden for most of the season. The key is to let nature do the work. For instance, rather than clean out and store away all my barren containers left over from fall, I group together those that are frost-proof into clusters, fill them with soil, and cover the tops with soft green moss. With an occasional watering, the moss stays colorful all winter. In containers such as my iron urn, I add lots of bright, berry-laden branches, and in others I pile up pinecones in a vivid winter display. To add a touch of green to my dormant borders, I assemble a collection of several small potted evergreens. Incorporating five different varieties of plants with contrasting forms and sizes, the composition holds my interest and needs no further embellishment. When I'm having guests over for dinner, I like to light their way to the door with votive candles. Glass holders suspended from branches of trees by simple wire hangers sparkle in the cold night air.

Here are several other ways to keep the winter landscape worthy of attention.

DON'T BE TOO TIDY. Rather than cleaning out everything from your borders, leave the stalks of ornamental grasses and plants with seed heads, and interesting winter forms. Personally, I prefer to leave most of my perennial foliage standing through the winter, cutting things back in very early spring, both for aesthetic reasons and to provide food and shelter for birds. However, there is some benefit to getting rid of some of the foliage, especially if your garden was troubled with fungus and disease during the growing season.

INVITE THE WILDLIFE. Few things add more winter cheer than lively squirrels and colorful birds feeding in the garden. When placing my feeders, I like to put them in areas where the wildlife will feel safe and I can still enjoy watching them from the windows. For wintering birds the best location for a feeder is about 10 feet from a large shrub or tree where they can take cover without predators bothering them. And I usually set up several feeding stations in different areas of my garden to help disperse the activity and prevent overcrowding.

LEFT *Crown weatherproof containers with a mound of soft moss to create a striking, yet simple covering for your empty winter containers.* **OPPOSITE** *Darkness comes early in winter, so when I invite guests for dinner, I light their way to my doorstep by hanging jam jar votives in trees.*

1. Boxwood and 'Needlepoint' holly
2. Pinecones
3. 'Harbor Dwarf' Nandina
4. River birch bark
5. Winterberry
6. Variegated Japanese silver grass
7. Red-stemmed dogwood
8. Framed vegetable beds
9. Leatherleaf mahonia

Winter Interest

Although it may be too late to plant this year, now's the time to make a list of what you would like to add next spring to jazz up your winter garden. There are categories of plants that go unnoticed during the growing seasons when more-colorful flowers and foliage grab all the attention. As the palette changes in winter, these plants step forward to claim center stage, due to their winter color or interesting shapes.

1.
2.
3.
4.
5.
6.
7.
8.
9.

EVERGREENS. Often acting as the neutral backdrop for more-colorful flowers, evergreens blend into the tapestry of a summer garden. In winter they take on more prominence, adding a reassuring shade of green to an otherwise stark landscape. Both needled and broad-leaved evergreens add substantial mass and form.

ARCHITECTURAL PLANTS. Plants that have strong forms and distinctive shapes, either in the nature of their leaves, such as a yucca (*Yucca flaccida*), or in their overall growth pattern, like a corkscrew willow (*Salix matsudana* 'Tortuosa'), are referred to as architectural plants. They can serve as focal points in the winter landscape.

BARK AND COLORFUL BRANCHES. Concealed behind a veil of green foliage during the spring and summer, plants with unusual bark, such as paper birch (*Betula papyrifera*) or sycamore trees (*Platanus occidentalis*), are standouts once the leaves have fallen. Shrubs with brightly colored branches, like red- and yellow-twig dogwoods (*Cornus stolonifera*), as well as those with unique textures add eye-catching appeal.

BERRIES. I consider berries the flowers of winter. Not only do they add color to the garden, they provide food for birds as well. Gleaming like bright ornaments adorning trees and shrubs, they come in a variety of colors from deep purple to scarlet, orange, and yellow. Nandina (*Nandina domestica*), winterberry (*Ilex verticillata*), beautyberry (*Callicarpa* spp.), and pyracantha (*Pyracanta* spp.) are just a few examples.

GROUND COVERS. As the leaves fall away from trees, shrubs, and flower beds, evergreen foliage becomes more noticeable and more cherished, and none so much as the ground covers that keep the bare earth green during the darkening days of winter. Evergreen low-growing plants are beautiful additions to a winter garden. These plants add a carpet of color, pattern, and texture to otherwise bare spots in your flower beds and banks. Pachysandra, ajuga, and wintercreeper (*Euonymus fortunei*) are just a few of the choices.

BLOOMS. If you live in mild areas of the country, you can enjoy the beauty of flowers in your winter landscape. Cool-season bloomers such as pansies and violas shake off the snow and temperatures that dip below freezing to keep right on flowering. Early-blooming plants such as hellebores and winter jasmine are the first brave soldiers to appear after the New Year.

STRUCTURES. Though not a group of plants, constructed objects play a big role in defining the framework of my garden. Pathways, fences, fountains, tuteurs, arbors, trellises, statues, planter boxes, pots, containers, birdhouses, buildings, and benches are all examples of outdoor structures that lend dimension to my winter landscape.

ABOVE *Metal open-weave urns lined with moss hold an arrangement of winterberry branches (*Ilex verticillata*) and help to brighten the entrance to my loggia.* LEFT *A collection of small conical evergreens and a moss-covered wire basket arranged on a table is an easy way to make a seasonal display that will last through the holidays and beyond.* OPPOSITE, ABOVE *Hellebores bloom in late December and early January, bringing life and color to the winter garden.* OPPOSITE, BELOW *The stark lines of this black iron urn silhouetted against the winter landscape allow me to appreciate its artful form.*

ABOVE AND RIGHT *Serve up a beautiful holiday centerpiece by packing in several 'Red Lion' amaryllis bulbs "shoulder to shoulder" in a large container. Once they bloom, slip the container into a more decorative holder, like this large silver bowl, and cover the base with holly leaves, berries, and juniper foliage.* **ABOVE RIGHT** *After the holidays I enjoy having fresh amaryllis flowers blooming throughout the house, but choose varieties in colors other than red, such as this striking cream and burgundy bloom of the butterfly amaryllis (*Hippeastrum papilio*).*

Winter Bouquets

As the color drains from the landscape and winter winds rattle my windows, I long for a few fresh flowers to remind me of warmer days in the garden. Cut flowers from the florist are always a nice pick-me-up, but I find it's also enjoyable to grow my own blooms from bulbs. Amaryllis and paperwhites are two varieties that are so easy to grow that once I get started, it's hard to stop. Amaryllis will bloom in 6 to 8 weeks and paperwhite bulbs will flower in some 4 weeks. I like to keep the flowers coming all winter, so I stagger my plantings and pot up a few bulbs about twice a month.

Amaryllis

Amaryllis is considered to be the king of the indoor flowers. One look at the giant trumpet-shaped blooms of varieties such as 'Red Lion' and you'll agree the flower is aptly named. Along with Trumpet amaryllis, there are also varieties with fanciful spidery blooms called Cybisters. That's why amaryllis are so addictive to grow—you can choose from so many different bloom styles and colors and a range of plant heights. While the large-flowering, red with white star, 22-inch-tall 'Minerva' makes a bold statement on the buffet in my dining room, for a bedside table in a guest room, I find the miniature, white with bright green center flowers of the 16-inch 'Green Goddess' to be just right.

During the holidays I go for richly hued blooms in dramatic sizes and then change to lighter shades such as 'Lemon Lime', with its sparkling white petals, after the New Year. A single bulb planted in a decorative pot with a bit of sheet moss covering the soil is a stylish accent. Or you can make a bolder statement by packing several bulbs together. Amaryllis can also be combined with other forced blooms such as paperwhites, hyacinths, and tulips for a late-winter/early-spring garden.

When it comes to selecting amaryllis bulbs, it's helpful to know that larger bulbs do make a difference in bloom size. The 20- to 24-cm bulbs (they are graded by the number of centimeters around the bulb) will often produce two stalks per bulb. A 28-cm bulb will develop two stems and sometimes three. When you consider that each stalk can be crowned with two to five flowers, you can understand why the amaryllis is considered to be such an outstanding indoor flower.

There are just a few basics to know about growing an amaryllis. Simply place the bulb in a container that is a few inches wider than the bulb. Fill the container with soil, leaving approximately one-quarter of the bulb exposed. Water and place it in a sunny location. After a few weeks a long stalk will emerge, followed by a beautiful flower. It's important to have plenty of stakes on hand to give the flower stalk a little support because the blooms grow so large that they become top-heavy and topple over, breaking the stalk. While your amaryllis is in bloom, water when the soil is dry and keep the plant away from sources of heat such as air vents and fireplaces to ensure that the blooms last.

Once your amaryllis finishes flowering, cut off the stalk, but leave the foliage. This will help reinvigorate the bulb so you will have plenty of blooms next year. During the non-blooming part of its life, treat it like an ordinary houseplant. Keep its foliage alive to restore energy to the bulb. And then in mid-October cut back the foliage, put it in a dark place, and stop watering. About a month later bring it out and place it in a location that gets full sun and begin watering it again. Soon you'll be enjoying a whole new generation of flowers.

Paperwhites

Since paperwhites take less time to flower than amaryllis, I usually wait until just before Thanksgiving to start potting up the bulbs so I'll have flowers in time for Christmas. I never tire of these winter-blooming narcissus. Their pure white blossoms and fragrant petals add a sweet freshness to my holiday decorating, although not everyone finds their fragrance so endearing.

Like amaryllis, the bulbs don't need to be

prechilled, so all you need to do is pot them up and they'll start to grow. Buy only firm, shiny brown-coated bulbs and purchase enough to plant new pots every 2 weeks for a steady supply of flowers through the winter. Store the unplanted bulbs in a brown paper bag in a cool, dry location. Because they don't require any soil to grow, some of your stored bulbs may begin to sprout and send up shoots. Handle these carefully, and plant those with the longest shoots first.

Paperwhites will grow in almost anything—soil, gravel, or just plain water. I have grown them in clear vases with glass beads and water so I could see the whole plant, roots and all, develop. However, my preference is to plant them in soil because the bulbs are thus well anchored and they tip over less frequently. If you prefer gravel, fill the container roughly two-thirds with the gravel, nestle the bulb in until about half is covered, and then add water just to the top of the gravel.

When I plant the bulbs in soil, I fill the pot about two-thirds with moistened potting soil, push the bulbs in, and add more soil to cover the bulbs, leaving approximately 1 inch of the top of the bulb uncovered. Keep the planted bulbs in a warm, light place and growth will begin immediately. A 5-inch pot will hold 3 or 4 bulbs, snuggled against each other. If they touch, it's fine. The effect when they bloom will be of a bouquet emerging from the pot. Sometimes I top the soil with rye grass seeds, which will sprout in no time, creating a mini-meadow scene.

Keep the plants well watered, and watch the shoots turn green and lengthen. Buds emerge in 3 weeks or so, and blooms will follow a week later. To keep them looking their best, display the flowers in cool locations. Left at room temperatures, the shoots elongate and make the pots top-heavy. Pretty much the only problem with paperwhites is that they can grow tall and spindly and have a tendency to flop over; to avoid this, give them plenty of light and turn the container 180 degrees each day. If the light source is too faint or far away, the plant will strain toward the light, making the stems weak.

If set in a cool place like a sheltered porch where temperatures are in the 40s and 50s, the blooms can go on for 3 weeks. However, they can't take freezing temperatures and they will expire quickly if set in an area with temperatures in the 30s.

My favorite variety is called 'Ziva'. The petals and cups are white and the fragrance is sweet rather than musky. The fragrance of different kinds of paperwhites varies. All seem to get a stronger aroma once they are past their prime. There are several paperwhite varieties to choose from that go beyond the standard white. Here is a short list.

RIGHT *Paperwhites are most captivating when grouped together in a cluster to create a bouquet of blooms.* **OPPOSITE** *During mild stretches in the winter, I like to bring my paperwhites out on my covered porch. Like most flowers, the blooms last much longer in temperatures that are cooler than a heated house.*

'CHINESE SACRED LILY' White petals with an orange-yellow cup. Grows 12 to 20 inches and may need staking. Wonderful fragrance.

'CONSTANTINOPLE' A double form of 'Chinese Sacred Lily' with white petals and an orange-yellow cup. Grows 12 to 20 inches. Sweet fragrance.

'GRAND SOLEIL D'OR' Yellow petals with an orange cup. Grows 12 to 14 inches. Sweet fragrance.

'GOLDEN RAIN' Double mutation from 'Grand Soleil d'Or' with similar fragrance and coloration; a rare find from a grower in Cornwall, England. Grows 12 to 14 inches. Sweet fragrance.

'JERUSALEM' Very large, white petals and cup. Grows 16 to 20 inches. Moderate fragrance.

'NAZARETH' Pale yellow petals with a vibrant yellow cup. Grows 10 to 12 inches. Moderate fragrance.

Paperwhite Pageantry

After growing paperwhites for a few years, I have discovered that they have a chameleon-like quality that makes them fun to use in a variety of arrangements. I like to add them as elements to create a number of mini-scenes on tables and sideboards. Grouped with pinecones, cut boughs, candles, and apples, I can count on their tall flourishes of flowers to give my compositions a lift. And since they bloom for weeks, I don't have to change them out as frequently as cut flowers. Another time-saving feature I like about paperwhites is that unlike some holiday plants such as poinsettias that look passé after the holidays, the blooms of paperwhites fit into my home's decor before and after Christmas, giving me more time to use and enjoy them.

There are a few tricks I've learned in creating these displays.

- For some arrangements, I find they look best combined with contrasting elements such as sprigs of holly, cedar boughs, and candles. The flowers seem to pop when they are arranged with colors and textures that are different from the paperwhite's.
- Since I like to keep fresh blooms coming, I pot up a batch of bulbs every 2 weeks or so. At times I run out of containers to put them in, so I just start them in 8-inch-diameter nursery pots. That's when I pack in lots of bulbs for a big show of blooms. Once they are up and growing, all I need to do is slip them into a more decorative container. The mass of flowers makes a simple but striking focal point.
- Other times I use smaller 4-inch nursery pots and put just a few bulbs in each one. Then I line the pots up in a long, low basket and cover the tops with sheet moss. This elongates the display, perfect for a table or entry hall arrangement.
- Along with sheet moss, I've also used small pinecones to help conceal and lend interest to the top of the container. The added texture is a fun way to bring another element of design to the arrangement.
- The standard way to give paperwhites a little help in standing tall is to insert slender sticks next to the flower stalks. As an alternative approach, I found several lichen-covered branches and poked them into the container's soil and then gently wove the flower stalks within them. The twigs imparted a casual, woodsy feel to the display.
- Another variation on the theme of adding support to keep a bouquet of paperwhites upright is to incorporate a tall edging around the inside of the container. I bend supple twigs into overlapping hoops to create a tall scalloped effect.
- And if you want to try to shorten the length of the stems, here's a recipe to try. Start your bulbs in plain water and when the stems are 1 to 2 inches long, drain the water and replace it with a solution of 1 part gin (or vodka) to 7 parts water. As the stalks grow, they'll be shorter and less likely to bend. Seems a fitting recipe around the holidays!

ABOVE LEFT *A cocktail of gin and water applied to emerging paperwhites stunts the lengths of the stems and prevents the plants from becoming top-heavy when the flowers open.* **LEFT** *Bending supple stems into hoops set around the edge of a container creates a quick and attractive way to prop up paperwhites' flower stems.* **OPPOSITE** *Lichen-covered branches contrast nicely with the paperwhites' delicate blossoms and serve as supports to keep the long flower stalks standing tall. Mixing several other types of textures into this arrangement, such as Granny Smith apples, pinecones, and evergreens also adds visual interest.*

winter wildlife garden party

There is such a crush of holiday activities leading up to Christmas that I wanted to come up with a fresh way to invite guests over for a seasonal celebration. So in recent years, I've started a new tradition of throwing a garden party in early December. When guests arrive, they get into the spirit by joining me in decorating the garden to attract local wildlife. The festive decorations we create double as edible treats.

To set a celebratory mood for the party, I do a little pre-decorating in the garden. Both guests and feathered friends are greeted at the door with a wreath decorated in dried fruit slices and berry ornaments accented with mini terra-cotta pots filled with suet. I also like to wrap garlands around the entryway columns of the arbors. To save time and money, I've found a neat little shortcut that turns inexpensive artificial garlands into something grand. I buy several long strands and cover them with clusters of bundled live evergreen stems. Then I wire on accents of pinecones, seed heads, and berried branches to give them more color and interest.

materials

6- to 8-inch stems of live evergreen boughs (cedar, pine, fir, juniper, spruce, boxwood, bay laurel, and, in some regions, eucalyptus)
Pruners
Florist wire
Artificial garland
Wire cutters or heavy scissors
Branches of berried limbs (holly, nandina, rose hips, viburnum, bayberry)
Pinecones

1. With the hand pruners, clip off several 6- to 8-inch lengths of evergreen boughs.

2. Create small bundles of evergreens by wiring handfuls of trimmings together.

3. Wire overlapping evergreen bundles onto the artificial garland.

4. Wire berried branches and pinecones as accents on the garland.

5. Wind and secure the garland around posts, columns, and deck and porch railings.

continues on following page

before guests arrive

Be sure to clear sidewalks and paths of any snow and ice. If you have an outdoor fireplace, portable fire pit, or chiminea, a warm fire would be a great addition. If it's very cold that day, it's also a good idea to set out a box of extra hats and scarves. To keep everyone in the holiday spirit, have some of your favorite holiday tunes on hand. And think about nighttime lighting if the party goes on into dusk.

Set up workstations on card tables filled with all the items your guests will need to be creative in assembling the decorations. Let your garden take the lead for gathering natural materials such as pinecones, evergreen boughs, berried branches (holly, nandina, rose hips), dried flowers, grasses, and seed heads. If you need extra evergreen boughs, consider purchasing a cut Christmas tree and prune it for its branches. You'll also need a supply of florist wire, string, and utensils. If children are joining the fun, ask some of the adults ahead of time if they would help supervise at each table to keep things safe. I find it's easier for people to get started if they have some finished ornaments to serve as a guide.

once guests arrive

Direct them to the tables so they can begin to make the decorations. Some can start stringing cranberries and popcorn, others can tie together bundles of evergreens and berried branches and add loops of strings to make them easy to attach to trees and shrubs. Making the suet-filled orange baskets and bread round ornaments is always a hit. I've found that people gravitate to the activities they enjoy.

While the decorations are being assembled, some guests help me give an unassuming, bare-branched "Charlie Brown" tree the star treatment as we adorn it with strands of cranberries and popcorn, dried apple and orange slices, bread circles threaded on raffia, dried flower heads, and orange baskets, creating a veritable smorgasbord for birds. To fashion a holder for the tree, I wrap a bucket with burlap and fill it with wet sand and gravel. To make the "tree," I gather sturdy bare branches and arrange them in the bucket, patting the sand around the base of the branches to make them nice and sturdy in the holder. I surround the tree with a mini-forest of young cypress trees potted in simple frost-proof containers. Along with decorating the tree, partygoers are encouraged to deck out every corner of the garden with fruity strands and nutty garlands, all delicious treats for birds and squirrels.

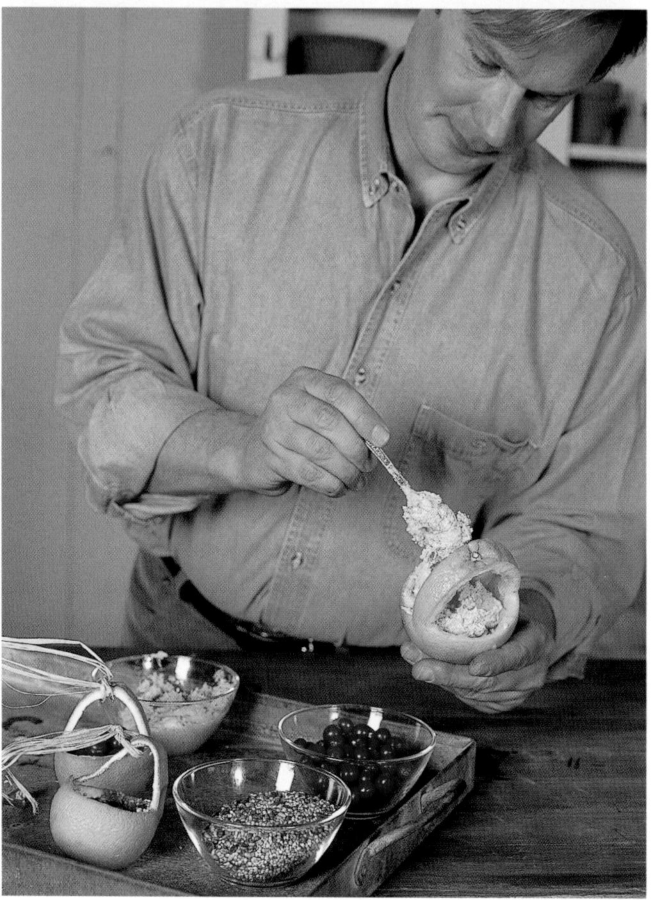

suet-filled orange baskets

It's fun putting these little suet-filled orange baskets together, and the birds will enjoy the feast all winter long. I've discovered that things go more smoothly if the orange baskets are cut ahead of time and the suet is ready to be added to the baskets, especially if children are involved.

materials

10 oranges
Wide rubber bands
Fine-tipped marking pen
Sharp knife
Spoon
1 cup peanut butter
1 cup shortening (or lard)
1 to 2 cups oatmeal or cornmeal
1 cup birdseed

1. Soften the shortening and peanut butter in a pan over low heat.

2. Stir in the oatmeal and birdseed. Let cool.

3. Wrap an orange with a wide rubber band. With a marker, start in the middle of the orange and trace a line along the top edge of the band, ending in the middle of the orange on the opposite side. Draw an identical line along the bottom edge of the rubber band.

4. Remove the rubber band and use a sharp knife to carve a "handle" out of the top half of the orange following the marked lines. Keep the area that was under the rubber band intact and cut away the rest, leaving the bottom half of the orange as the basket.

5. Scoop the pulp out of the orange.

6. Spoon the suet into the orange baskets and sprinkle extra birdseed on top. Add a string or piece of raffia to tie the ornaments on the tree.

hot mulled cider

I set up my nearby loggia with hot drinks and snacks so everyone can take a break and admire their work. Along with warm dips, appetizers, and crackers, I like to serve hot mulled cider. It's the perfect drink on a cold day and its spicy aroma fills the air.

INGREDIENTS

2 quarts apple juice or apple cider
2 cups orange juice
1 cup pineapple juice
½ cup lemon juice
½ cup brown sugar
2 cinnamon sticks
2 teaspoons cloves
1 teaspoon allspice
1 teaspoon powdered ginger
orange slices for garnish

1. Combine the juices in a large pot. You can substitute apple cider for the apple juice if you would prefer. The cider makes it a bit effervescent. Add the brown sugar, cinnamon sticks, cloves, allspice, and powdered ginger. Cook the mixture over medium heat until it begins to boil, and then reduce the heat and let it simmer about 15 minutes longer.

2. Pour the drink into a serving container such as a punch bowl. Garnish it with a few fresh orange slices. This recipe makes enough for ten 1-cup servings. As you can imagine, with all of these spices, the aroma is incredible.

Simple gifts from the Garden

To spread holiday cheer to special friends and neighbors, I enjoy creating distinctive seasonal decorations that they may not have time to make themselves. Filling friends' window boxes or planters with boughs, berries, and fruit is a way to brighten their homes. If you live where winter temperatures stay below freezing, fill the planter boxes with cut material, such as evergreen boughs and branches, so the display will last for weeks. In milder areas, cold-hardy plants such as pansies, violas, and ornamental kale will last through the winter. Use your imagination and materials from your area to make your own regionally unique design.

fruits of winter planter box

- Bag of small apples
- Winterberry branches
- Bucket of pinecones
- Spruce and fir branches
- Cedar branches with blue berries
- Pruners
- Antitranspirant (available at garden centers)

1. Treat the evergreen boughs with antitranspirant. Follow label directions.

2. Create a nest of evergreen boughs to spill over the edge of the box.

3. Cut lengths of berried branches to accent the evergreens.

4. Layer in bright red apples and pinecones to finish the display. In cool, above-freezing temperatures, the apples should last a week or so. If temperatures regularly dip below freezing, use red ornaments in place of the apples.

PLANT MATERIAL FOR OTHER COLD-HARDY ARRANGEMENTS

- **Boughs of evergreens:** pine, eastern cedar, fir, spruce, yews, holly, boxwood
- **Berried and colorful branches:** winterberry, silverberry, rose hips, red- and yellow-stem dogwood
- **Accents:** pinecones, bayberry, dried hydrangea blossoms, seed heads of ornamental grasses

Winter wreaths

Holiday wreaths are timeless decorations that reflect the spirit of the season. The circle is a symbol of wholeness and continuity, and because wreaths are often made of evergreen material, they also represent everlasting life, both enduring messages during the holiday season. Whether you lean toward traditional styles or the latest in avant-garde, wreaths can be crafted to complement any décor.

moss wreath

Here's a beautiful alternative to an evergreen wreath that you can enjoy for months. The soft gray color of the moss goes with any color scheme, and the chocolate velvet bow dresses up the wreath but keeps it in style as a seasonal accent even after the holidays.

materials

1 large bag of reindeer moss or lichen
16-inch grapevine wreath
Large bow
Hot glue gun and glue sticks
Floral U-pins
Floral wire
Bucket with water
Large bowl

1. Moisten a few handfuls of the lichen or moss in the bucket of water to make them more pliable and easy to work with. Put them in the large bowl.

2. Place the grapevine wreath on a flat surface. Before gluing pieces of moss to the wreath, position them on it to determine the size and arrangement for the best coverage.

3. Begin adding hot glue to the back side of the moss pieces and press them onto the wreath. Continue working until the front and sides are covered with moss. In addition to the hot glue, use floral U-pins or pieces of floral wire bent in a U shape to securely attach the moss to the wreath.

4. Wire on the bow and add a loop of ribbon at the top to use as a hanger for the wreath.

WINTER WREATH TIP

Before using the greenery, soak wreaths, garlands, and boughs overnight, completely submerged in water. I have some galvanized tubs in my garage for this, but a bathtub will also work.

berried beauty

When I'm designing my garden and I want a particular area to truly stand out, I plant large drifts of a single variety of plant. For example, when I plant tulips in the fall I select varieties of the same color family and really pack in the bulbs. For the best visual impact, my motto is the more the better. And the same is true in holiday decorating.

Rather than sprinkling a few red berries on a green wreath, why not cover the wreath with berries for a bold impact? To create this wreath, gather up a few supplies: a foam wreath form, floral wire, clippers, floral U-pins, and lots of branches of berries. This wreath requires a lot of berries, so you may want to select a small wreath form and make sure you have enough berries to cover it.

First make the bundles of red berries. For this wreath, I used the gorgeous red berries of a Chinese photinia, which is a southern plant. For northern gardeners, try rose hips or winterberries. The point is, don't worry if you can't find the same type of berries; see what's available at the florist, from a craft store, or in your garden and get something that appeals to you. To make the bundles, gather three to five stems, cutting the ends to make them even, and tie them together with floral wire. Working your way around the wreath, pin the bundles on the foam using floral U-pins, overlapping the bundles as you go. Before you know it, you'll have encircled the entire wreath. If you'd like, you can add a bow as a final accent, but I like the strong and striking berries to speak for themselves.

lemon eucalyptus wreath

Accent a silvery eucalyptus wreath with bright yellow lemons for a fresh and fragrant design. I used an 18-inch artificial wreath with branches made of flexible wire for the foundation. That's handy because you can twist and bend the branches, making it easy to attach the eucalyptus All you'll need to get started is some floral wire, an ice pick, scissors, floral wire, clippers, a large green velvet bow, 20 seeded eucalyptus branches (depending on their size), 9 lemons, and boughs of traditional greenery of your choice.

Cover the artificial wreath by wiring bundles of clipped evergreens on top. I used Leyland cypress from my garden, but just about any kind of evergreen will do. The live greenery will cover the artificial wreath and provides nice textural contrast to the eucalyptus. Next insert the ends of the eucalyptus into the frame of the wreath and tie them down with the wire stems of the artificial wreath. Layer the eucalyptus around the wreath, placing the branches all in the same direction in an overlapping fashion. Pierce the lemons near the top with an ice pick and push an 8-inch length of floral wire through the hole. Securely attach the lemons to the wreath using the wire. Then just tie on a big bow.

granny smith apple wreath

Start with a fresh fir or spruce wreath from the garden center and embellish it with things you have on hand. I wired bundles of juniper branches and some Chinese photinia foliage to plump up the volume of the wreath. Then "pre-drill" a hole through the center of 15 Granny Smith apples with an ice pick and run covered florist wire (from your local craft store) through the apples. (At first I tried to use green pipe cleaners but found that premeasured lengths of florist wire were longer and easier to slip through the apples. The coating on the wire keeps it from slicing through the apple while they are hanging on the wreath.) I gathered up some of my dried hydrangea blossoms that I clipped from my bushes last summer. As they air-dried they were left with a slight green cast which looked nice against the evergreen wreath. Others dried to a soft tan; I wanted to give them a little extra color, so I sprayed them with a light green floral spray. You can do the same or pick up hydrangea blossoms of your choice at a craft or florist shop.

While you are there, pick up some green hypericum berries. To prepare them for use, strip off the foliage and then wire the berry sprigs and the apples securely on the wreath. I wasn't sure how long the berries would hold up without water, but they lasted a couple of weeks. I think it helped to remove the foliage.

Holiday Tree Traditions

When European immigrants settled in this country, they brought with them their practice of using an evergreen tree as a symbol of their Christian beliefs. The idea for the Christmas tree is rooted in the Middle Ages with what was called the paradise tree. Apples, representing the Garden of Eden, were hung on a fir tree. Because it was an evergreen, it stood for Eternal Life. The apples themselves harken back to Adam and Eve and the Tree of Knowledge, but the Germans were the ones who brought the tree indoors as the centerpiece of the celebration. They are largely responsible for the custom as we know it today. Children of all ages get excited about Christmas trees. Bringing a little of the outdoors, or nature, inside always seems to stir the imagination.

Tips when buying a cut tree:

- Inspect the stump where the tree was cut. The sap, or pitch, should be soft and sticky. If it's hard and dry, the tree is not fresh. Go on to the next tree.
- Stand the tree upright and bounce it to loosen the branches. Only a few needles should fall off. If you are showered with needles, look for another tree.
- Check the twigs and needles. Recently cut trees should have soft and flexible tips. Look inside—older cut trees will start to lose their needles from the inside up and out toward the branch tips.
- When you get your tree home, recut the trunk so the end is fresh and can take up water; I also score the end with a hatchet to help the tree draw up more moisture before I put it into its stand.
- Once you have your presents piled around the tree, it's hard to keep the tree stand full of water. An easy solution is that when the water gets low, drop a few ice cubes in the stand and let them melt.

KEEPING EVERGREENS GREEN

If you're a holiday traditionalist like me, you probably opt for a real tree and fresh greenery. There's no substitute for their beauty and aroma. However, keeping evergreens fresh can be a challenge, particularly if you like to decorate early.

The key to keeping greenery vibrant, whether it's a garland, a wreath, or an entire tree, is to keep moisture in the stems, leaves, or needles. That can be done two ways. First, make sure whatever you purchase is as fresh as possible. Look for a rich green color, flexible stems, and little needle drop.

Plants naturally lose water through their stems and leaves through a process called transpiration, and an antitranspirant can be used to seal plant pores to minimize water loss. Greenery can be treated at the nursery or you can buy various brands of antitranspirants at the garden center and apply them yourself at home. Be sure to let the evergeens dry a few hours before you begin decorating. Treating your evergreens this way will keep them fresh longer.

holiday centerpieces

In keeping with the theme of using what's on hand, I've come up with several centerpieces made from things I could find in my garden or at the supermarket. When I don't feel like decorating an entire room, I've found that a single centerpiece is all I need to set a festive mood. I use them in my foyer, on a coffee table, in a guest room, or as a centerpiece on the dining room table. Take a look at these ideas and modify them to utilize what you can find close by. Grab some flowers, clip a handful of branches, buy a few sacks of fruit, and pull out any ornaments or decorative containers in your cupboard. You can also look beyond your own garden for seasonal materials. Floral shops, craft and grocery stores, and garden centers may be sources. Friends and neighbors may also be willing to let you gather items from their gardens. The important thing is to have some fun.

frosted fruit centerpiece

December is such a busy month that there's little time to decorate for the season, let alone come up with new ideas. So why not take a tried-and-true technique, such as turning colorful fruits into a frosty sugar-glazed presentation? The sugar-coated fruit add an elegant accent to garlands, wreaths, and tabletop decorations, and it takes only three ingredients: fruit, egg whites, and sugar. Sugar-coated apples, pears, limes, lemons, grapes, and kumquats, along with sprigs of Douglas fir, are piled high on a footed cake plate to create this striking presentation.

materials

Assortment of fruit (grapes, pears, apples, limes, lemons, kumquats)
Sprigs of Douglas fir (or other evergreen)
Footed glass cake plate
12-inch block of floral foam
Floral clay or tape
Floral picks
Egg whites from 6 eggs
Sugar
Waxed paper

1. Start by shaping a block of floral foam into a flat-topped cone. Secure the cone to a raised plate using floral clay or floral tape.

2. Insert picks into the largest pieces of fruit and brush them with the egg whites. Gently roll the fruit into granulated sugar to completely coat it and then set it on waxed paper to let the pieces dry overnight.

3. The next day, start at the bottom of the cone and anchor the larger pieces of sugared fruit by pressing the picks into the foam. Equally distribute the various kinds of fruit around the cone.

4. Fill in with smaller pieces, like the grapes, and add fir sprigs in between the fruit as a final accent.

You can expect the display to last 7 to 10 days. After the holidays, take the fruit outside and hang it from the trees. What a great dessert for the birds!

Tip: If you are in a hurry, spray adhesive can be used instead of egg whites. Just be sure not to eat the fruit or offer it to the birds after it is sprayed. And to make the fruit easier to adhere to the cone, slice off pieces to flatten one side of the fruit.

variegated poinsettia centerpiece

These 'Strawberries and Cream' poinsettias are a welcome change from the traditional red. New colors of this classic holiday plant make it easy to find one that will match your home's decor. There are also some great new patterns that create added interest. Some poinsettia leaves are blotched and speckled, while others look as though they've been frosted with color. Experiment with these new varieties to create your own version of this arrangement.

- 'Strawberries and Cream' poinsettias
- Leyland cypress
- Pinecones glued to floral picks
- Hypericum berries
- Water picks
- Bronze icicle ornaments
- Bronze ball ornaments
- Gold ribbon

Just slip the potted plants into a low basket and then fill it up with whatever you have on hand. Make sure the basket has a liner so you can water your poinsettias. Slip in small pieces of floral foam to help anchor the other elements. Fill around the poinsettias with stems of evergreens such as Leyland cypress, pinecones glued to floral picks, hypericum berries, copper-colored ornaments, and strips of gold ribbon. What could be easier?

Tip: The hypericum berries will last longer if you slide them into small water-filled floral vials. Anchor the vials in the floral foam wedged in between the pots, camouflaging them among the leaves.

white winter roses centerpiece

Simple and elegant, all it takes is a few white roses and freesia to create this stylish arrangement. No one will guess that you threw it together in minutes. Many grocery stores offer beautiful flowers. When you are picking up food for dinner, grab some roses and freesia. Look through your cupboard for a seldom-used item such as a sugar bowl or soup tureen to serve as the container.

- White spray roses
- White freesia
- Variegated English holly
- Western cedar
- Gold icicle ornaments
- Glass icicle ornaments
- Gold ball ornaments (optional)
- Floral foam
- Floral clay or tape

Anchor a cut block of presoaked floral foam to the bottom of the container using floral clay or tape. Make sure the foam doesn't show above the top of the container. Anchor in the roses and freesia, and a few clipped sprigs of variegated holly and cedar. Stick in some sparkling icicle ornaments. Add water and call it done.

Tip: Use holiday tree ornaments in arrangements to add sparkle.

produce-aisle centerpiece

One trip down the produce section of your grocery store is about all you'll need to gather the ingredients for this centerpiece. Colorful red apples and Anjou pears draped with stringed cranberries are combined with aromatic stems of western red cedar and Douglas fir. A few cinnamon-scented pinecones are mixed in for a polished, sweet-scented display. Apply cinnamon-scented oil to the cones using a Q-tip.

- Anjou pears (red and green)
- Red apples
- Pinecones glued to floral picks
- Stringed cranberries (or wooden ones)
- Western cedar boughs
- Douglas fir boughs
- Container of choice
- Floral foam
- Florist tape or clay
- Floral picks
- Hot glue gun and glue sticks
- Cinnamon-scented oil
- Q-tips

Cut a block of floral foam to fit inside the container. Soak it in water for an hour or so to thoroughly saturate the block. Tape the block, or use floral clay, to secure it inside the container. Pierce the fruit with wooden floral picks and anchor them into the foam. Hot-glue the pinecones to the wooden floral picks and insert them into the foam. Fill in between the fruit and pinecones with sprigs of cedar. Drape the stringed cranberries through the arrangement.

Tip: To give the fruit a long-lasting shine, coat each piece with vegetable spray.

curly red poinsettia and artichoke centerpiece

Artichokes aren't the typical accent found in holiday displays, but in this case their large dramatic form makes the perfect complement to the curly-leafed 'Winter Red Rose' poinsettia and the smooth, glossy Granny Smith apples. Think about creating interesting contrasts when choosing items for your centerpiece. The textural difference between these materials is what makes the composition so captivating.

- 'Winter Red Rose' poinsettia
- Artichokes
- Granny Smith apples
- Western cedar
- Twigs spray-painted gold
- Terra-cotta pot
- Floral foam
- Floral tape
- Wooden floral picks
- Ice pick

Tape a piece of presoaked floral foam into the terra-cotta pot. Pierce the apples and artichokes with wooden floral picks and anchor them into the foam. Leave room for the poinsettia branches. Cover the top of the terra-cotta pot with sprigs of western cedar. Cut stems of 'Winter Red Rose' poinsettia and arrange them between the apples and artichokes. Fill in small gaps with additional sprigs of cedar. For a bit of sparkle, add golden twigs as a bright accent.

Tip: Use a match to burn the end of a cut poinsettia stem for a few seconds to prevent sap from seeping.

mini-gardens under glass

After the holidays and while I'm waiting for those first signs of new life in the garden, I get a little itchy to put some plants in the ground. One year my niece and nephew were over for a visit and we decided to put together a mini-garden in a terrarium. It was a delightful afternoon project. Once planted and covered, a terrarium practically takes care of itself. The plants inside the glass enclosure create their own microclimate, producing moisture that condenses on the glass and then flows back into the soil.

materials

Wide-mouth glass container

Something to cover the jar top such as clear plastic wrap, a pane of glass, or Plexiglas

Potting soil

Small plants (see list below)

Aquarium gravel

Watering can or spray bottle

GOOD TERRARIUM PLANTS

- Acorus
- Aluminum plant (*Pilea cadierii*)
- Creeping fig (*Ficus pumila*)
- Moss
- Maidenhair spleenwort (*Asplenium trichomanes*)
- 'Needlepoint' ivy (*Hedera helix* 'Needlepoint')
- Oxalis
- Peperomia
- Prayer plant (*Maranta leuconeura*)
- Peacock moss (*Selaginella uncinata*)

1. Select a container for the terrarium. For easy access, pick one that has a wide mouth. A fishbowl or an aquarium is a good choice. I used an apothecary jar with a glass top. If your container does not have a lid, you can cover it with clear plastic wrap, a piece of clear Plexiglas, or a sheet of glass.

2. To avoid insect and disease problems, wash the gravel with hot water and use top-quality, sterile potting soil.

3. Fill the bottom of the container with about 1 inch of gravel. If your container is especially deep, you may want to use another inch or so of gravel.

4. Top the gravel with 3 inches of soil.

5. Now comes the fun part: planting the landscape. When you choose plants, select varieties that all have the same growing requirements—light, water, and humidity. Slow growers with small leaves are best suited for the confines of a terrarium.

Remove the plants from their pots and plant them in the terrarium just like you would in the garden. Place the taller plants in the back, midsize plants in the middle, and low-growing things like moss toward the front. If possible, keep the foliage away from the sides of the container.

6. Once you have the plants in place, moisten the soil lightly and put the lid in place.

How often you will need to water your terrarium depends on how tightly the lid fits. A good indication of when to water is the condensation on the glass. If there is no condensation, water the soil very lightly. If there is heavy condensation, remove the lid to allow the terrarium to air out.

The neat thing about terrariums is that you are only limited by your imagination. Add large rocks to represent craggy mountains or small mirrors for ponds. You can even create a desert landscape with succulents and cacti.

march
april
may
june
july
august
september
october
november
december
january
february

LATE WINTER

Mail-Order Catalogs

A harbinger of spring is when my mail-order gardening catalogs start to arrive. They begin to appear the day after New Year's, and before I know it, there are stacks piled up around my chair. It's a moment in the gardening year I always relish. There's nothing more enjoyable than curling up in my favorite reading chair with a hot cup of coffee and thumbing through the pages of my favorite plant catalogs. Everything seems possible as I marvel at all the new plant introductions and let my imagination fly with all the new dreams I have for my spring garden.

Here are just a few of my favorite catalogs.

- THE ANTIQUE ROSE EMPORIUM—For those who love old-fashioned roses, this is the catalog for you. You'll drool over the beautiful full-color rose photos and find the cultural descriptions helpful in selecting the variety best suited for your area.
- BEAUTY FROM BULBS—John Scheepers offers more than 750 varieties of tulips, narcissi, lilies, amaryllis, and rare and unusual Dutch bulbs. Since I like to buy large spring-flowering bulbs in bulk, the company's large volume discounts are especially attractive to me. Scheepers also has a great Kitchen Garden Seeds catalog.
- BLUESTONE PERENNIALS—I must admit, since I'm from a family of nurserymen, I like doing business with family-owned and -operated companies. Bluestone is a long-established mail-order supplier of more than 900 varieties of quality perennials and shrubs.
- BRENT AND BECKY'S BULBS—True bulb experts, this company knows the best bulbs for American gardens. Lots of varieties and great service make it a reliable source.
- FERRY-MORSE SEED & CO.—Not only does this long-established firm offer more than 750 varieties of seeds, but it also has all of the Jiffy seed-starter products that make it so simple to propagate your own seeds indoors.
- GILBERT H. WILD & SON—America's largest grower of daylilies, irises, and peonies has more than 400 acres packed with lots of varieties. Plants are dug by hand from the field the day before they are shipped. I had the pleasure of visiting the growing fields in Sarcoxie, Missouri, to see the peonies when they were in full bloom. Amazing!
- KLEHM'S SONG SPARROW FARM AND NURSERY—This wonderful Wisconsin nursery offers homegrown peonies, tree peonies, daylilies, clematis, hostas, unique perennials, shrubs, dwarf conifers, and small trees. It is especially noted for its exceptional peonies.
- McCLURE & ZIMMERMAN—This bulb catalog has lots of cultural information that makes it much easier to choose the right selections. The company has a great assortment and the bulbs are fully guaranteed.
- PEACEFUL VALLEY FARM SUPPLY—I like to support companies that provide products for sustainable agricultural practices. This firm was one of the very first in the country to offer organic supplies, and it now carries a wide variety of products, including pest control, seeds, fertilizers, and books.
- SCHREINER'S—This is a dwarf, beardless, and bearded iris lover's catalog for sure. Schreiner's has been in the iris business for over 75 years and has won plenty of awards for developing amazing colors and styles of iris to show for it.
- WILDSEED FARMS—If you are into wildflowers, this is the catalog for you. The catalog features more than 90 different varieties of wildflowers, native grasses, regional wildflower mixes, exotic garden varieties, and herbs.

Winter Pruning

By now, I'm more than eager to get outdoors and get the ball rolling on some pre-spring projects. Before the saps starts to rise in dormant plants, it's time to prune. This task is generally one of the first things I do in my garden to prepare for the growing season. Since I have many varieties of roses in my garden, it takes a few days to prune them all, so I like to get started in February.

Depending on your disposition, pruning roses can be seen as either the final task of winter or the first activity of spring. Either way, roses should be pruned just before they come out of dormancy and put out new growth.

Roses come in many forms, but whether you are growing a hybrid tea or an old-fashioned climber, pruning is basically the same for each type. The hardest part is making the first cut.

It's important to prune because it encourages healthy, vigorous stem growth. If you stop to think about it, it just makes sense. Stronger stems result in larger blooms, while spindly growth will produce smaller roses. It also removes dead, frost-damaged, and diseased wood, which lays the groundwork for a healthy growing season, and it opens the center of the plant, promoting good air circulation, which is essential for healthy roses. Pruning helps maintain an attractive and well-balanced shape to the plant as well.

The Right Cut

For shrub and climbing roses, make your cuts at a 45-degree angle, about ¼ inch above an outward-facing bud. The position of the bud on the cane indicates the direction of the new growth. By carefully selecting which bud becomes the stem producer you can manipulate the shape of the rosebush.

Climbing roses bloom mainly on laterals that grow from the canes. In order to encourage them to put out more flowering laterals, train the canes as horizontally as possible. The strong climbing shoots (canes) should be trained to fan out horizontally without allowing shoots to cross each other.

Once-blooming climbing roses should not be pruned now, as they flower only once a year on wood from the previous season. Prune these roses right after flowering is finished. Young climbers (including climbing miniatures) under 2 to 3 years old should be pruned lightly or not at all. Now is the time to prune repeat-blooming climbers. If it is a grafted rose, remove all suckers coming from below the bud union. Remove all dead or twiggy growth extending from the bud union. Cut all the flowering laterals that arise from the horizontal growing canes back to two or three buds. Remove all remaining leaves. Untie canes and reposition them on their support into as horizontal a position as possible.

For shrub roses, begin by removing dead and diseased wood. Small stems can be cut back with your hand pruners; use your loppers on larger canes. The next thing to do is to remove any large, old canes and cut them at the base of the plant.

Once the plant is cleaned up, take a close look at its form. Pick out three or four of the strongest canes and remove the others. Now cut back about one-third of the top growth and any crisscrossing stems to promote good air circulation. Take out stems that are smaller than the diameter of a pencil.

Remove any leaves left on the plant from last year. This will help prevent carrying over black spot and other fungi and pests. To finish the job, pick up all the resulting debris, bag it, and throw it away.

Signs of Winter's End

Color starved and winter weary, I often go into my garden in early February in search of any new signs of life. I'm always happy to see timid tips of daffodil foliage poking up in the borders and swollen leaf buds holding some promise that spring is not far away. But my heart leaps when I come upon a flower in bloom—a solitary ground-hugging crocus or the bright yellow blossoms of winter jasmine is such a thrill. But what excites me the most is when my hellebores, or Lenten roses, begin to bloom. It is a sight I anticipate all winter long.

HELLEBORES. *Helleborus* x *hybridus* is one of nature's great acts of restraint and sophistication. The pendulous, saucer-shaped blooms are a real eye-catcher in the late-winter early-spring garden. Because it flowers around the time of Lent, there is little to outstage its subtle beauty. Even after the flowers fade, the leathery, dark green foliage adds great texture to the garden. And if deer resistance is critical to you, these plants are a must. Because they are toxic, deer and other wildlife avoid them. However, this characteristic should be kept in mind if you have pets or small children. Be sure to plant hellebores where they are not easily accessible.

There are several species and varieties of hellebores that I find enticing. Although you can find fancier hybrids, my favorites are those that are cream to chartreuse in color or the deep purple-black varieties. When I was at the Portland (Oregon) Home and Garden Show, I picked up a black hellebore and cradled it in my lap for the entire flight back home. I was delighted to see the deep maroon flowers emerge. Unfortunately, I can't remember the cultivar name, but that will soon be remedied. C. Colston Burrell and Judith Knott Tyler have written what I can safely say is the definitive book on hellebores. Chock-full of growing guidelines, hybridizing tips, and design advice, this book will reveal everything you need to know about this beautiful winter-blooming plant. (See Suggested Reading, page 213.)

In addition to *H.* x *hybridus* I have also grown *H. foetidus,* or stinking hellebore. As the name implies, when the leaves are crushed they smell quite unpleasant, but the bell-shaped green blooms edged in purple are lovely and typically have a sweet scent. *H. niger,* or Christmas rose, is another favorite. Large white blooms that fade to pink are produced close to Christmas in my garden, making it one of the earliest plants to bloom.

Hybrid hellebores come in a wide range of colors from black to apricot to green. Some are even speckled or blotched. The flower forms to choose from include single petaled, double, and anemone. One word of caution: Named hybrids will vary from plant to plant, so to ensure that you get the color and form that you desire, purchase the plant when it is in bloom so that you can see the flower.

You'll find hellebores to be a versatile plant, thriving in both full sun and full shade, although I have had the best luck when I plant them in partial shade. They also prefer to be planted shallow so the top of the root ball is just below the surface in well-drained soil. Mine have proved to be quite drought resistant, and they seem to do best when watered as the soil becomes dry. Wet feet are the kiss of death for them.

Hellebores require very little fertilizing, but I like to work a shovelful of well-rotted manure or compost into the soil around the plant every few years. Although I enjoy the evergreen foliage through most of the year, I cut it back in late January to make room for the blooms and new emerging leaves.

As you attempt to grow this unique perennial in your flower borders, be patient. It can be hard to establish in your garden, although well worth any trouble. Once happy, it will be with you for years to come, requiring little care. And an added bonus is that hellebores make excellent, long-lasting cut flowers to enjoy indoors.

CAMELLIAS. Another plant that is one of my long-time favorite late-winter/early-spring-flowering shrubs is the camellia. *Camellia sasanqua* is one of the finest blooming shrubs that I grow in my garden and the harbinger of its later-flowering and better-known cousin, *C. japonica.* While *C. japonica* blooms with the characteristic large flowers, *C.*

OPPOSITE *With shy, nodding heads, hellebores are one of the first flowers to break through winter's gloom. Originally the perennials were residents of central Europe. Now they adorn gardens across America with translucent flowers of many different tones. To get the color best suited for your garden, select varieties while they are in bloom.*

ABOVE *'La Peppermint' camellia (*Camellia japonica*) is one of the stars of my late-winter garden. It's an old French variety from the 1800s that I found at a nursery in Louisiana. As spring progresses the flowers will taper off and the shrub will slip into the background, serving as a dark green canvas for summer's perennials, roses, and annuals.* **RIGHT** *Make an instant centerpiece by placing freshly cut blooms into jam jars nestled inside a basket.*

sasanqua is covered with loads of smaller blooms. If you live in the South or parts of the country that have mild winters similar to California's, you are probably familiar with these plants.

If you live in other parts of the country, visit your garden center to see if some of the new, cold-hardy varieties are being offered. These are thanks to work that has been done at the National Arboretum in Washington, D.C. Through an extensive breeding program the staff there have come up with several varieties that are actually very cold hardy, able to withstand the winters in places like New England and the Midwest.

To further ensure a successful experience when growing camellias in colder climates, plant them in a sheltered area that receives bright but filtered light. They prefer naturally acidic soils, but you can also apply fertilizer developed especially for camellias. A 3- to 4-inch layer of mulch will help keep the roots from freezing; just be sure to keep the mulch away from the trunk of the shrub. I find that when it comes to feeding these plants, it's best to apply fertilizer shortly after the blooms fade.

Now, don't despair if you live where you can't enjoy camellias outdoors. Many of them make excellent container plants for a greenhouse, atrium, or garden room. Growing them this way can give you an even better chance to enjoy their beauty up close.

Once those first, brave pioneers of spring appear—witch hazel, snowdrops, crocuses, hellebores, camellias, and winter jasmine—it's time to say farewell to winter and I turn to embrace a new growing year. I find the repeating seasons to be such a comfort—soothing rhythms that I can count on in our ever changing, fast-paced culture. During the ups and downs of daily living, knowing that I can return to my garden to reconnect to the eternal, deeper forces of nature gives me great peace. And so I've come full circle in my gardening year. Happily, it is a circle, and I'm ready to go around again.

Here are a few of the spring-blooming, cold-hardy camellias available and the two parent plants that were crossed to develop the winter-tolerant variety.

- **'Betty Sette'** *C. japonica* 'Frost Queen' x *C. japonica* 'Variety Z'. Compact, upright, average growth rate. Leaves broad, glossy, dark green. Flowers medium pink, formal double of good substance. Late. Cold hardy to –10 degrees F.
- **'Cream Puff'** *C. japonica* 'Frost Queen' x *C. japonica* 'White Butterfly'. Vigorous, upright growth. Leaves glossy, dished, very dark green. Flowers white, large, semidouble to loose peony, with good substance. Midseason to late. Cold hardy to –4 degrees F.
- **'Frost Queen'** Field trial selection from seed introduced from northern Japan. Dense, upright growth. Leaves glossy, dished, very dark green. Flowers white, large, semidouble with good substance. Midseason to late. Cold hardy to –4 degrees F.
- **'Ice Follies'** *C.* x *williamsii* 'November Pink' x *C. oleifera* 'Lu Shan Snow'. Open, spreading growth. Leaves dark green, semiglossy. Flowers bright pink, large, semidouble, crepelike petals. Blooms March–April. Cold hardy to –4 degrees F.
- **'Jerry Hill'** *C. japonica* 'Frost Queen' x *C. japonica* 'Variety Z'. Average, dense, upright growth. Leaves broad, glossy, dark green. Flowers rose pink, formal double. Late. Cold hardy to –10 degrees F.
- **'Londontown'** *C. japonica* 'Bertha A. Harmes' x *C. oleifera* 'Plain Jane'. Moderately vigorous, upright growth. Flowers deep red-pink, semidouble to loose peony, notched petals. Blooms March–April. Cold hardy to -4 degrees F.
- **'Pink Icicle'** *C.* x *williamsii* 'November Pink' x *C. oleifera* 'Lu Shan Snow'. Average, compact, upright growth. Leaves dark green, glossy. Flowers shell pink, large to very large, peony form with large rabbit ears. Blooms February–March. Cold hardy to –4 degrees F.
- **'Spring Frill'** *C. oleifera* 'Plain Jane' x *C. vernalis* 'Egao'. Slow, spreading growth. Leaves dull, medium green. Flowers bright iridescent pink, large, rose form double. Blooms April–May. Cold hardy to –10 degrees F.

source guide

SEEDS

Ferry-Morse Seed Co.
601 Stephen Beale Drive
Fulton, KY 42041
1-800-283-3400
www.ferry-morse.com

Franchi Sementi
PO Box 149
Winchester, MA 01890
1-781-721-5904
www.growitalian.com

Ivy Garth Seeds & Plants, Inc.
8410 Mayfield Road
Chesterland, OH 44026
1-800-351-4025
www.ivygarth.com

Johnny's Selected Seeds
955 Benton Avenue
Winslow, ME 04901
1-877-564-6697
www.johnnyseeds.com

Pennington Seed
PO Box 290
Madison, GA 30650
www.penningtonseed.com
(grass seed)

Renee's Garden Seeds
7389 W. Zayante Road
Felton, CA 95018
1-888-880-7228
www.reneesgarden.com

Seeds of Change
PO Box 15700
Santa Fe, NM 87592-1500
1-888-762-7333
www.seedsofchange.com

Select Seeds
180 Stickney Hill Road
Union, CT 06076-4617
1-800-684-0395
www.selectseeds.com

Thomas Jefferson Center
for Historic Plants
PO Box 316
Charlottesville, VA 22902
Orders: 1-800-243-1743
Customer Service: 1-800-243-0743
monticellostore.stores.yahoo.net/plants

Wildseed Farms
100 Legacy Drive
PO Box 3000
Fredericksburg, TX 78624-3000
1-800-848-0078
www.wildseedfarms.com

BULBS

B&D Lilies
PO Box 2007
Port Townsend, WA 98368
1-360-765-4341
www.lilybulb.com

Breck's
PO Box 65
Guilford, IN 47022
1-513-354-1511
www.brecks.com

Brent and Becky's Bulbs
7900 Daffodil Lane
Gloucester, VA 23061
1-877-661-2852
www.brentandbeckysbulbs.com

Colorblends
Schipper & Company
1-888-847-8637
www.colorblends.com

Daffodil Mart
Route 3, Box 794
Glouchester, VA 23061
1-804-693-3966
www.daffodilmart.com
(daffodil breeders and specialists)

Dutch Gardens
PO Box 400
Montvale, NJ 07645
1-201-391-4366
(many types of bulbs)

John Scheepers, Inc.
23 Tulip Drive
PO Box 638
Bantam, CT 06750-0638
1-860-567-0838
www.johnscheepers.com

McClure & Zimmerman
PO Box 368
Friesland, WI 53935-0368
1-800-883-6998
www.mzbulb.com

Rex Bulb Farm
Box 774
Port Townsend, WA 98368
1-206- 385-4280
(specializes in lilies)

Swan Island Dahlias
PO Box 700
Canby, OR 97013
1-800-410-6540
www.dahlias.com

Ty Ty Plantation
Box 159
Ty Ty, GA 31795
1-912-382-0404
(specializes in cannas, amaryllis, lilies, and tender bulbs)

Van Bourgondien & Sons, Inc.
PO Box 2000
Virginia Beach, VA 23450
1-800-622-9997
www.dutchbulbs.com

PLANTS

The Antique Rose Emporium
9300 Lueckemeyer Road
Brenham, TX 77833-6453
1-800-441-0002
www.antiqueroseemporium.com
(heritage roses)

Barry Glick
Sunshine Farm and Gardens
HC 67 Box 539 B
Renick, WV 24966
1-304-497-2208
www.sunfarm.com
(hellebores)

Bluestone Perennials, Inc.
7211 Middle Ridge Road
Madison, OH 44057
1-800-852-5243
www.bluestoneperennials.com

Gilbert H. Wild & Son, Inc.
PO Box 338
Sarcoxie, MO 64862
1-888-449-4537
www.gilberthwild.com
(daylilies, irises, and peonies)

Goodwin Creek Gardens
PO Box 83
Williams, OR 97544
1-888-846-7359
www.goodwincreekgardens.com

Greenwood Nursery
PO Box 686
McMinnville, TN 37111
1-800-426-0958
www.greenwoodnursery.com

Klehm's Song Sparrow Farm and Nursery
13101 East Rye Road
Avalon, WI 53505
1-800-553-3715
www.songsparrow.com

Logee's Greenhouses
141 North Street
Danielson, CT 06239-1939
1-888-330-8038
www.logees.com

Nourse Farms
41 River Road
South Deerfield, MA 01373
1-413-665-2658
www.noursefarms.com

Oakes Daylilies
PO Box 268
Corryton, TN 37721
1-800-532-9545
www.oakesdaylilies.com

Plant Delights Nursery, Inc.
9241 Sauls Road
Raleigh, NC 27603
1-919-772-4794
www.plantdelights.com

Proven Winners
111 East Elm Street, Suite D
Sycamore, IL 60178
1-877-865-5818
www.provenwinners.com
(annuals and perennials)

Roots & Rhizomes
PO Box 9
Randolph, WI 53956-0009
1-800-374-5035
www.rootsrhizomes.com

Roslyn Nursery
211 Burrs Lane
Dix Hills, NY 11746
1-631-643-9347
www.roslynnursery.com
(cold-hardy camellias; catalogs are $3.00)

Schreiner's Iris Gardens
3625 Quinaby Road NE
Salem, OR 97303
1-800-525-2367
(mail-order iris)

Stokes Tropicals
4806 East Old Spanish Trail
Jeanerette, LA 70544
1-866-478-2502
www.stokestropicals.com

Wayside Gardens
1 Garden Lane
Hodges, SC 29695-0001
1-800-213-0379
www.waysidegardens.com

White Flower Farm
PO Box 50
Litchfield, CT 06759-0050
1-800-503-9624
www.whiteflowerfarm.com

CONTAINERS AND PLANTER BOXES

Braun Horticulture
1-800-246-6984
www.braungroup.com
(hypertufa containers)

New England Pottery
1000 Washington St.
Foxboro, MA 02035
1-800-666-6614
www.nepottery.com
(pottery containers)

Nichols Bros. Stoneworks, Ltd.
20209 Broadway
Snonomish, WA 98296
nicholsbros.com
(stone containers)

Norcal Pottery Products, Inc.
PO Box 1628
2091 Williams St.
San Leandro, CA 94577
1-877-722-3592
www.norcalpottery.com
(pottery containers)

PROJECT SUPPLIES

Bonny Doon Farm
600 Martin Road
Santa Cruz, CA 95060
1-831-459-0957
info@bonnydoonfarm.com
www.bonnydoonfarm.com
(lavender products)

Green Piece Wire Art
PO Box 260
Bridge Station
Niagara Falls, NY 14305
1-877-956-5901
www.greenpiecewireart.com
(wire animal topiaries)

Matthews Four Seasons
6677 East Hardaway Road
Stockton, CA 95215
1-800-755-1757
www.matthewsfourseasons.com
(quality wood garden products)

Sugar Plum Farms
1263 Isaac Branch Road
Plumtree, NC 28665
1-888-257-0019
www.sugarplumfarms.com
(Christmas trees and cut greenery)

HERITAGE APPLES

Applesource
Order online or by fax
Fax: 217- 245-7844
www.applesource.com
(mail-order heritage apples)

Big Horse Creek Farm
PO Box 70
Lansing, NC 28643
1-336-384-1134
www.bighorsecreekfarm.com
(over 200 varieties available; good descriptions in the catalog)

Orchard Lane Growers
5014 Orchard Lane
Gloucester, VA 23061
1-804-694-0470
(wide selection of heritage varieties)

Trees of Antiquity (previously Sonoma Antique Apple Nursery)
20 Wellsona Road
Paso Robles, CA 93446
1-805-467-9909
www.treesofantiquity.com
(about 150 varieties available; very informative catalog)

TOOLS

Fiskars Garden and Outdoor Living
780 Carolina St.
Sauk City, WI 53583
1-800-500-4849
www.fiskars.com

LIGHTING

Circa Lighting
405 Whitaker St.
Savannah, GA 31401
1-877-762-2323
www.circalighting.com

Deep Landing Workshop
115 Deep Landing Road
Chestertown, MD 21620
1-410-778-4042
1-877-778-4042
deepland@dmv.com
www.deeplandingworkshop.com

Gardener's Supply Company
128 Intervale Road
Burlington, VT 05401
1-800-427-3363
www.gardeners.com
(garden supplies including milky spores)

SOIL/SOIL AMENDMENTS

Nutrimoist
American Soil Technologies, Inc.
1-800-798-7645
www.americansoiltech.com
(water-retentive polymers)

Peaceful Valley Farm and Garden Supply
PO Box 2209
Clydesdale Court
Grass Valley, CA 95945
1-888-784-1722
www.groworganic.com
(organic garden supplies, including milky spores)

Premier Horticultural Soils—Pro-Mix
1-215-529-1290
www.premierhort.com
(high-performance growing mediums)

PAINT

Sherwin-Williams
www.sherwin-williams.com (for store locator nearest you)

OUTDOOR FURNITURE

Barlow Tyrie
1263 Glen Ave.
Suite 230
Moorestown, NY 08057
1-800-451-7467
www.teak.com

Country Casual
7601 Rickenbacker Dr.
Gaithersburg, MD 20879
1-800-289-8325
www.countrycasual.com

Laneventure
PO Box 849
Conover, NC 28613
1-800-235-3558
www.laneventure.com

McKinnon & Harris
1806 Summit Ave.
Richmond, VA 23230
1-804-358-2385
www.mckinnonharris.com

Summer Classics
PO Box 390
7000 Highway 25
Montevallo, AL 35115
1-205-987-3100
www.summerclassics.com

OUTDOOR STRUCTURES

Cedarworks
799 Commercial St.
PO Box 990
Rockport, ME 04856
1-937-587-2656
customerservice@cedar-works.com
www.cedar-works.com
(bird feeders)

Walpole Woodworkers
767 East St., Rte. 27
Walpole, MA 02081
1-800-343-6948
www.walpolewoodworkers.com
(handcrafted gates, fences, arbors, etc.)

FABRIC

Sunbrella
Glen Raven, Inc.
Glen Raven Custom Fabrics, LLC
Attn: Customer Service
1831 North Park Ave.
Glen Raven, NC 27217
1-336-227-2211
www.sunbrella.com

suggested reading

Allison, Christine. *365 Days of Gardening*. New York: HarperCollins, 1995.

Armitage, Allan. *Armitage's Garden Annuals: A Color Encyclopedia*. Portland, OR: Timber Press, 2004.

Austin, Claire. *Irises: A Gardener's Encyclopedia*. Portland, OR: Timber Press, 2005.

Beutler, Linda. *Gardening with Clematis: Design and Cultivation*. Portland, OR: Timber Press, 2004.

Bubel, Nancy. *Nancy Bubel's Handbook of Garden Projects for All Seasons*. New York: Rodale, 1993.

Burrell, C. Colston, and Judith Knott Tyler. *Hellebores: A Comprehensive Guide*. Portland, OR: Timber Press, 2006.

Chatto, Beth. *Beth Chatto's Garden Notebook*. Portland, OR: Sagapress, Inc., 1997.

———. *Beth Chatto's Green Tapestry*. New York: HarperCollins, 1999.

———. *The Damp Garden*. Portland, OR: Sagapress, Inc., 1993.

———. *The Dry Garden*. Portland, OR: Sagapress, Inc., 1996.

Clebsch, Betsy. *The New Book of Salvias: Sages for Every Garden*. Portland, OR: Timber Press, 2003.

Cooke, Ian. *The Gardener's Guide to Growing Cannas*. Portland, OR: Timber Press, 2001.

Darke, Rick. *The Color Encyclopedia of Ornamental Grasses: Sedges, Rushes, Restios, Cat-tails, and Selected Bamboos*. Portland, OR: Timber Press, 1999.

DiSabato-Aust, Tracy. *The Well-Designed Mixed Garden: Building Beds and Borders with Trees, Shrubs, Perennials, Annuals, and Bulbs*. Portland, OR: Timber Press, 2003.

———. *The Well-Tended Perennial Garden: Planting and Pruning Techniques*. Portland, OR: Timber Press, 2006.

Don, Montagu. *The Sensuous Garden*. New York: Simon & Schuster, 1997.

Editors of Storey Publishing's Country Wisdom Boards. *Country Wisdom & Know-How*. New York: Black Dog & Leventhal Publishers, 2004.

Goodwin, Nancy. *Montrose: Life in a Garden*. Durham, NC: Duke University Press, 2005.

Gordon, Robert, and Sydney Eddison. *Monet the Gardener*. New York: Universe Publishing, 2002.

Grenfell, Diana, and Mike Shadrack. *The Color Encyclopedia of Hostas*. Portland, OR: Timber Press, 2004.

Heims, Dan, and Grahame Ware. *Heucheras and Heucherellas: Coral Bells and Foamy Bells*. Portland, OR: Timber Press, 2005.

Hillier, Malcolm. *Malcolm Hillier's Color Garden*. New York: Dorling Kindersley, 1995.

Hobhouse, Penelope. *Colour in Your Garden*. London: Frances Lincoln Ltd., 1985.

Lawson, Andrew. *The Gardener's Book of Color*. London: Frances Lincoln Ltd., 1996.

Lloyd, Christopher. *The Well-Tempered Garden*. New York: Viking, 1985.

Loewer, Peter. *The Evening Garden*. Portland, OR: Timber Press, 2002.

McHoy, Peter. *Pruning: A Practical Guide*. New York: Abbeville Press, 1993.

Macoboy, Stirling. *The Illustrated Encyclopedia of Camellias*. Portland, OR: Timber Press, 1998.

Nold, Robert. *Columbines: Aquilegia, Paraquilegia, and Semi-aquilegia.* Portland, OR: Timber Press, 2003.

Oudolf, Piet, and Henk Gerritsen. *Planting the Natural Garden.* Portland, OR: Timber Press, 2003.

Oudolf, Piet, and Michael King. *Gardening with Grasses.* Portland, OR: Timber Press, Inc., 1998.

Oudolf, Piet, and Noël Kingsbury. *Designing with Plants.* Portland, OR: Timber Press, 1999.

Peat, John P., and Ted L. Petit. *The Daylily: A Guide for Gardeners.* Portland, OR: Timber Press, 2004.

Pope, Nori, and Sandra Pope. *Color by Design.* London: Conran Octopus Ltd., 1998.

Reich, Lee. *The Pruning Book.* Newtown, CT: Taunton Press, 1997.

Rogers, Allan. *Peonies.* Portland, OR: Timber Press, 1995.

Schmid, George. *An Encyclopedia of Shade Perennials.* Portland, OR: Timber Press, 2002.

———. *Timber Press Pocket Guide to Shade Perennials.* Portland, OR: Timber Press, 2005.

Segall, Barbara. *The Herb Garden Month-by-Month,* Newton Abbot, Devon: David & Charles, 1997.

Staub, Jack. *75 Exciting Vegetables for Your Garden.* Layton, UT: Gibbs Smith, 2005.

acknowledgments

This book endeavors to connect the seasons to our daily lives, and while it is brought to life by the ideas, text, and photographs found on these pages, it is really the many talented people involved in its creation that gives it soul. For this I am grateful to a host of contributors.

I thank Betsy Lyman for her unwavering dedication to this book and the entire Garden Home series. Without the extraordinary talents of photographers Jane Colclasure and Kelly Quinn the activities and ideas described here would not be nearly as inspiring; their artful gaze framed each picture to capture its essence. I am also grateful to Betty Freeze for her countless hours of coordinating and organizing the plants and materials as well as her dedication to meticulous record keeping; Mary Ellen Pyle for crafting descriptions of many of the projects and for proofing the manuscript; Amy Bowers and Catherine Gilbert for collecting and coordinating the photography; and Sheb Fisher for her assistance in styling.

I'd also like to thank the many people at Clarkson Potter whose guidance and support made this book such a feast for the eyes, especially publisher Lauren Shakely and editorial director Doris Cooper. Much credit is due to the team of talented people who shaped the book into its final form, including editor Amy Pierpont and her assistant Lindsay Miller, art directors Marysarah Quinn and Jane Treuhaft, and book designer Dina Dell'Arciprete; to Mark McCauslin and Joan Denman for guiding the book along the production path; and to Tina Constable, Kate Tyler, and Campbell Wharton for trumpeting the word about the book through their promotional efforts.

I also owe many thanks to all the members of my staff at Hortus Ltd. who contribute greatly to the growth and success of our company: Elba Benitz, David Curran, David Duncan, Catherine Gilbert, Justin Haase, Pam Holden, Cindy Howenstein, Laura Leech, Gabe Mayhan, Todd Orr, Bill Reishtein, Suzanne Selby, and Mandy Shoptaw. And in remembrance of Frances Cheshire, I want to acknowledge her thorough and steadfast abilities to catalog and organize thousands of photographs for this and other publications; she will be missed.

I am fortunate to have such wonderful friends (of all ages) and clients who have generously given of their time and talents in support of this endeavor, including Susan, Rich, Graceleigh, and Sawyer Wright; JP, Ericka, Julian, and Sophie Francoeur; Fran Bollinger; Lee Ann and Isaac Bollinger; Anthony Shoptaw; Kelly Freeze; Teri and Ray Bunce; Andrew P. Walker; Ken Hughes; Brian Hardin; Shannon Blaylock; Rachael Freeze-Ramsey; Warren and Harriet Stephens; Sally Foley; Carl Miller, Jr.; Rick Smith and Susan Sims Smith; Kim and Mark Brockinton; Cheri and Mark Nichols; Nancy and Duncan Porter; Jim Dyke and Helen Porter; Cathy Hamilton Mayton and Mike Mayton; Charlotte and Robert Brown; Jim and Nancy Goodwin; Reed and Becky Thompson; Kelle Mills; Gaye and Robert Anderson; Ann West; Ken and Ellen Hughes; Randy Jeffery; Henry and Marilyn Lile; Doug Bradford; Kathy Graves; Rebecca and Gary Smith; Tricia Fowler; Sue Williamson; members of the Little Rock Garden Club; Somers Matthews and Andy Collins; Miles Slarks; Martha Melkovitz; Ari and Justin Mitchell; and Margaret Litton.

My gratitude also extends to the many companies that have been instrumental in supporting this book, including Sunbrella, Laneventure, Fiskars Garden and Outdoor Living, Matthews Four Seasons, Premier Horticultural Soils-Pro-Mix, Nutrimoist, Norcal Pottery Products, New England Pottery, Proven Winners, Central Garden and Pet, Ferry-Morse Seed Company, Sherwin-Williams, Pennington Seed, Pleasant View Gardens, Klehm's Song Sparrow Farm and Nursery, Applesource, Cantrell Gardens, Old Gin Antiques, Southern Wholesale Florists, Boulevard Bread Company, Culberson's Greenhouse, Hocott's Nursery, Vagabond Vintage Furnishings, Cobblestone and Vine, Arkansas Flag and Banner, and Bray Sheet Metal.

My appreciation also extends to the associates on my design team for their talents and ability to help me create new gardens: Ward Lile, Nicole Claas, Sarah Burr, Antonio Cruz, Josh Lindsey, Wes Parsons, Chris Ison, Steve Lindsey, Mario Tavarez, David Morris, Gene Morris, and especially my brother, Chris Smith, who is always there to keep things moving forward.

index

Note: Page numbers in *italic* indicate captions.

Sal
Tropical plants
hangea
Tulip

Roses
Lettuce
Lilies